going natural
natural
with
herbs

going natural with herbs

INTEGRATING HERBS INTO EVERYDAY USE

Maureen Kernion, M.S.

WOODLAND PUBLISHING
Pleasant Grove, Utah

©1998
Woodland Publishing
P.O. Box 160
Pleasant Grove, Utah
84062

NOTE: The information contained in this book is not intended as
medical advice, but is for educational purposes only. It is not
intended to diagnose, treat, or prescribe, and does not replace
the services of a trained physician. It is assumed that the reader
will consult a medical or health professional if a serious health
problem is suspect. Niether Woodland Publishing nor the author
directly or indirectly dispenses medical advice or prescribes the
use of herbs, supplements, or other forms of treatment without
medical approval.

Cover and book design by John Bernhard

PRINTED IN THE UNITED STATES OF AMERICA

dedication

This book is dedicated to my teacher, Rhonda Kilgore, for starting me on the path to herbal health through education and support.

contents

foreword

In my thirty years of learning about and sharing herbs, there has always been a common misunderstanding: herbs are not just medicine—they are nutrient-rich foods that help the body reestablish optimal wellness.

Maureen Kernion's *Going Natural with Herbs* is a concise, easy-to-understand reference that helps clear the confusion about the role of herbs in achieving overall good health. Mrs. Kernion's book is well-referenced, with research gleaned from both current sources and those tucked away thousands of years in our past.

The current American lifestyle is under a frightening assault from dietary and environmental toxins. Rather than eliminating these dangerous poisons and replacing them with healthy, natural foods, we often suppress the symptoms of sickness with more chemicals in the form of prescription medicines.

Going Natural with Herbs provides the basis to begin and maintain a regimen of good health, and will help all of us think beyond the medical realm of suppressing symptoms and focus instead on strengthening our bodies with good foods—herbs—in order to achieve an optimal state of health.

Good health,
Jim Jenks, H.M.D.

a note from the author
first, the bad news ─────────

- Americans pay more for health care than citizens of any other country ($900 billion in 1993).[1]
- The United States has fallen behind sixteen other nations in regard to the average life expectancy.[2]
- The United Nations World Health Organization warns that "diseases of the rich" (cancer, heart attack, strokes, and other diseases in which diet and exercise play a part) are increasing as the customs of industrialized nations spread to other parts of the globe.[3]
- One hundred million Americans suffer from chronic illnesses such as arthritis, heart disease, cancer and diabetes, costing $425 billion a year in health care expenses. Another $234 billion are spent on indirect costs such as lost work days.[4]
- Americans consume over half of all drugs used in the world. Each year 2.4 billion prescriptions are written in the United States.[5]
- According to the Food and Drug Administration (FDA), two hundred thousand people die each year from adverse drug reactions.[6]
- One hundred fifty thousand to three hundred thousand Americans are injured or killed each year from medical negligence involving mistreated disease, surgeries, drug reactions, and misprescribed drugs.[7]
- Thirty-six percent of hospital admissions are caused by side effects of other treatments and 53 percent of all surgeries are unnecessary.[8]
- About 90 percent of patients who visit doctors have conditions that will either improve on their own or that are out of the reach of modern medicine's ability to solve.[9]

This does not paint a pretty picture. Disappointment in traditional medicine has given rise to an upsurge of interest in healthy alternatives. Many doctors practicing mainstream medicine are beginning to recognize the value of adding natural options to patient care.

now, the good news

- Ninety-two out of 125 mainstream medical schools today (like Harvard) offer courses in nontraditional healing methods.[10]
- Traditional agencies like the federal government's National Institutes of Health (NIH) are now recognizing once-scoffed-at treatments such as the "relaxation response" for chronic pain.
- The NIH has budgeted $12 million in 1998 for its Office of Complementary and Alternative Medicine.[11]
- *The New England Journal of Medicine* reports that one-third of all Americans use alternatives to traditional medicine. Herbal supplements are one of the most popular of alternatives and account for $3 billion in sales annually.[12]
- A study at Harvard Medical School found that Americans spent $14 billion on alternative therapies in 1990, representing 425 million visits.[13]
- About a dozen health-care insurance companies cover alternative therapies like acupuncture or homeopathy. According to a recent survey, 58 percent of HMOs (health maintenance organizations) say they plan to offer alternative therapies within the next one to two years and seventy percent reported a rise in patient requests for those options.[14]

Fortunately, times are changing. We are on the verge of a complete transformation of our health care in the United States. For a growing number of Americans, this transformation has already occurred.

Increasing numbers of people have sought natural alternatives to traditional health care and have found that true health is possible.

Natural approaches, such as herbal therapies, are a safe way to feed the body the nutrition it needs so that it can heal itself.

Most Americans live in a fast-paced world that our ancestors could never have even imagined. The stresses of constant time pressure, lifestyle choices and environmental toxins take a serious toll on health. Now, more than ever, we need to know how to make informed decisions so that we can achieve *vibrant health.*

It is my sincere hope that you will use this book as a tool to help you pursue the wealth of information and support available. Herbs are a great way to start a healthier approach to life and take responsibility for our health. Allow this book to help you get started and to help you take your next steps on the path to true health and greater joy in life.

Maureen Kernion, M.S.

FOOTNOTES

1. Health News and Views, *The Life Connection* (October 1996).
2. Ibid.
3. U.N. World Health Organization, *World Health Report* (1997).
4. *Journal of the American Medical Association* (November 13, 1996).
5. *Health News and Views,* The Life Connection (October 1996).
6. Rick Ansorge, "Living Long," *Daily News/Freedom News Service* (September 8, 1996) p. C1.
7. *Wall Street Journal* (Jan. 13, 1993).
8. *Let's Live* (Feb. 1995).
9. *New England Journal of Medicine* (Dec. 25, 1980).
10. *Association of American Medical Colleges Survey* (1996).
11. David Perlman, "New Journal to Review Alternative Medicine," *San Francisco Chronicle/Walton Sun* (January 10 ,1998).
12. Ibid.
13. "Keynote Speaker Calls for Mutual Medical Respect," *Health Foods Business* (May 1994).
14. *Landmark Healthcare Survey of 80 HMOs.*

acknowledgments

I'd like to thank heaven above for the support that my husband Brad has provided through the writing of this book. Without him, it would not have happened.

Thanks also go to Ann Marie Karl, Esq. for her invaluable advice, editing, creativity, and counsel.

It would be impossible to list all the kind deeds of technical support and encouragement provided by friends, family and colleagues. But I thank you all and appreciate your efforts.

I am also grateful for the blessings that turned a crucial health situation into an education and renewal.

introduction

overview

"Let your food be your medicine and your medicine be your food."
Hippocrates

to get started on herbs is easy, but to get the most out of taking herbs requires a more "holistic" approach. There is no "magic bullet" in herbs, just as there is no magic bullet in any other kind of food. For example, broccoli is wonderful food but it is impossible to live on broccoli alone. Optimal health requires a variety of nutrients from a variety of sources. And that's where herbs come into play. They are legitimate sources of food—but even better, they contain many of the vitamins and minerals that feed the whole body.

definition of holistic

The term "holistic" is derived from the word "whole." Essentially, when you take a holistic approach to achieving optimal health, individual symptoms are disregarded in favor of the health of the whole. We were created as a whole with all parts working together to accomplish miraculous feats. Health is not the absence of illness. Health is enjoying physical, spiritual, mental, and emotional well-being. When was the last time you felt really great in every way?

holistic health

A solid plan for total health includes a balance of many aspects of well-being. Achieving total health involves several important elements such as a healthy mental attitude, a healthy diet, rest, sunshine, physical/mental/spiritual exercise, healthy relationships, clean water, and clean air. Herbs can be an essential part of a healthy diet, but herbs and diet are only a piece of the puzzle. For example, the healthiest diet in the world won't mean much if we feel angry, bitter, or overly stressed. A body suffering from stress can't properly digest the food that it receives and, as a result, can't fully absorb the nutrients.

taking responsibility

Herbs allow you to take responsibility for your own health; they work as great preventive health care. Herbs can also be used in situations not serious enough to require medical care. More importantly, herbs can work hand in glove to form a health partnership with medical treatment to get the best of both worlds. If in doubt about whether to use herbs or medical treatments, always seek the advice and expertise (especially in the area of diagnosis) of a qualified health professional.

learning from other countries

We have much to learn from other countries. According to the World Health Organization, 80 percent of the people on Earth rely on herbal medicines.[1] German physicians, for example, write more prescriptions for St. John's wort for depression than any other prescription, including twenty-five times the amount they write for Prozac.[2] On the other hand, Prozac is the third leading prescription drug in America with $1.7 billion in sales.[3] Prozac has generated 28,623 adverse reaction reports to the Food and Drug Administration (FDA) as of October 1993. Complaints included 1,885 suicide attempts and 1,349 deaths and represent the largest number of complaints to the FDA.[4] We've made lots of progress in this country in the area of natural approaches, but we have a long way to go.

learning from our past

The ancient civilizations of China, Egypt, Rome, India, and Native America have documented the safe use of herbs throughout the centuries. We refer to health options such as herbs and homeopathic medicines as "alternative medicine." In many ways, though, the medical structure in America today is alternative—it is alternative to the medicine practiced for centuries in most of the world's cultures.

how to get the most out of this book

GENERAL FORMAT: This book is set up for easy-on-the-eyes reading and will hopefully be material that you'll want to keep for easy reference. Listed below are a few parts of the structure about which you'll want to make a mental note.

POWER PLANTS: "Power Plants" is a chapter dedicated to describing the historical uses of herbs along with some information on scientific studies performed on those herbs. Whenever an herb is mentioned in one of the other chapters, a superscript "PP" (*example:* ginseng[PP]) will appear to let you know that you can get more information about that herb in the "Power Plants" chapter.

FURTHER READING: Whenever appropriate, other publications regarding a particular subject will be mentioned so that if you are interested in more detailed information you can be pointed in that direction. The listing of a book does not mean that the author and/or publisher agree with every premise outlined in that book. Recommendations for further reading point out material that is very worthwhile to someone who is interested in more information on that topic. After reading with an open mind, decide for yourself what is right for you in your pursuit of healthy lifestyle avenues.

FOOD FOR THOUGHT: Periodically you'll see questions that can help you to take the ideas presented in the chapter and apply them to potential action items in your life.

final thoughts

We may have a long way to go to get back to basics. But an ever-increasing number of people are taking those first steps to join the ranks of those who used to be called "health nuts," but are now referred to as "health conscious." They are discovering for themselves the excitement of increased physical, mental and emotional energy through a natural approach to life.

FURTHER READING

Health and Healing, Andrew Weil, M.D., Houghton Mifflin, 1995.
Think and Be Healthy, by Jim Jenks, H.M.D., LJ Publishing, 1988.

FOOTNOTES

1. Louise Tenney, M.H., *The Encyclopedia of Natural Remedies*, p.1.
2. Sue Miller, "A Natural Mood Booster", *Newsweek* (May 5, 1997) pp.4-5 .
3. Bob, Condor, "Herbal Remedy May Offer New Solution to Old Problem," *Chicago Tribune/Daily News* (November 10,1997) p. C1-2.
4. Ann Blake Tracy, Ph.D., *Prozac: Panacea or Pandora?*, Cassia Publications, 1994.

who should read this book?

"The best time to do something is between yesterday and tomorrow."
Anonymous

are you considering using therapeutic herbs to get started on a healthier lifestyle but don't know where to start? Have you used herbs but are not sure you're getting the most benefit from them? Are you interested in some quick tips to help you create a healthier lifestyle for you or your family? Are you interested in some general health tips but can't find a concise source to get you started? This book is a perfect place to answer these questions. Let's get started.

what's in store

This book is designed to be a map to help you get started on therapeutic herbs with a holistic look at getting the most out of the herbs you take. If you're interested in any of the following topics, read on:

- ◆ What are herbs?
- ◆ Why bother to take herbs?
- ◆ How are herbs different from drugs?
- ◆ Who should take herbs?

- What forms and types of herbs are most effective for different circumstances?
- How and when to take herbs
- Herbs that flash the "caution" light
- Herbs to have on hand for emergencies and "urgencies"
- What to expect when you take herbs
- Which herbs feed which body systems
- Other natural health choices
- Where to go to find more information on different natural health topics

who should *not* read this book?

If you're expecting an overnight solution to all your problems, a pill to cure all ills, you won't find it here. What you will find are lots of different approaches that, with commitment over time, can make a big difference in your health.

final thoughts

The world of herbs combines a wealth of folklore with the validation of recent scientific studies. Welcome to the groundswell of reliance on herbs, nature's grocery store and treasure chest.

herbal basics

why should i?

"Thirty percent of the characteristics of aging are genetically determined, seventy percent [are] linked to lifestyle..."
John Rowe, M.D., Mt. Sinai Medical Center

i t is understandable that plunging into a different way of life is a frightening venture, a challenging departure from your everyday routine. But just in case you're not convinced that herbs are the path you want to choose, let's look at some compelling reasons for taking the herbal path to optimal wellness.

safety

In general, herbs have been used safely for thousands of years all over the world. Herbs and homeopathic* remedies were used here in the United States until the late nineteenth century when modern medicine became dominant.

nutrients

You may have heard doctors or nutritionists say that we don't need vitamin or mineral supplements, that we can get every nutrient we need from food. That may have been true before American soil became so depleted of nutrients and processed

* For more information, see the chapter on Other Natural Health Approaches.

food became the standard American diet. But more about that later. For now, we must understand doctors and nutritionists agree that nutrients are much better when obtained from food. And that's what herbs are—whole food. Vitamins and minerals are much more effective when nature balances the other nutrients that need to be combined in the right proportions in order to be effective. Iron, for example, needs vitamin C to be fully absorbed.

bioavailability

The degree to which nutrients are available for the body to break down, absorb, and use as fuel is called bioavailability. Herbs are very bioavailable because the body recognizes them as food. The body will not however recognize oyster shells (for calcium) or rusty nail shavings (used to fortify cereal with iron[1]) as a food. When we think about it, this comes, of course, as no shock. After all, many vitamin and mineral supplements are made with coal tar.[2] These are nutrients from the Earth, but they are hardly in a state our bodies can handle effectively. In fact, these synthetic nutrients may do more harm than good.

nutrient "insurance"

We have just begun to discover the value of nutrients in our food. Nutrients such as indoles and isoflavones are recent discoveries that seem to provide protection against diseases like cancer. Until we discover the individual components and determine which ones should and should not be isolated from the other nutrients in food, we're a lot safer eating whole, natural foods—like herbs.

a note on heredity

Some feel that heredity has locked them invariably into a life of malaise and "non-healthiness." You usually think something along the lines of "I'll always have poor circulation just like my father and his father." It is important to understand, however, that heredity is just a starting point for you on your pathway in life. Your outlook and attitude toward life, supplemented by your lifestyle and nutrition choices, can be detrimental to your health—or it may provide a solid starting point for a long and healthy life, regardless of heredity.

final thoughts

Because six of ten American deaths are related to diet,[3] we could use some nutrient insurance. Herbs are a great way to get power-packed nutrients to help you achieve optimal health.

FURTHER READING

Back to Basics with Herbs, by Jim Jenks, H.M.D., Woodland, 1984.

FOOTNOTES

1. Steven H. Horne, "Mineral Nutrition," *Healthwise* (Video), VI (November 1994).
2. James F. Balch, M.D. and Phyllis A. Balch, C.N.C., *Prescription for Nutritional Healing,* p. 13.
3. Phyllis A. Balch, C.N.C. and James F. Balch, M.D., *Prescription for Cooking and Dietary Wellness,* p. 2.

what are herbs?

"And God said, Behold, I have given you every herb-bearing seed, which is upon the face of all the earth..."
Genesis 1:29 KJV

have you ever eaten garlic[PP] because you heard it's good for your health, or in particular, your arteries? Have you chewed parsley[PP] after the garlic[PP] to freshen your breath? Have you eaten an after-dinner peppermint[PP] to settle your stomach? Have you had a cup of tea to help you concentrate? Have you ever used aloe vera[PP] on a burn? If you answered yes to any of these questions, you've used herbs.

definition

Webster's Ninth New Collegiate Dictionary defines the word "herb" as "a plant or plant part valued for its medicinal, savory, or aromatic qualities." Any mention of herbs in this book refers to plants or trees that have been used through the ages to bring balance to the body. Herbs are used to build and cleanse the body or to activate certain functions (like glandular functions). Herbs are a concentrated source of vitamins, minerals (especially trace minerals), enzymes, and other catalysts (like bioflavonoids) that make certain nutrients (like vitamin C) more effective.

herbal ABCs

Herbalist Edward Milo Millet is credited with coining the herbal ABC phrase to define the three basic functions of herbs. Following is a description of each function:

ACTIVATE: Some glands need to be activated. Kelp[PP], for example has been used to activate the thyroid for healthy metabolism and weight management.

BUILD: Some systems of the body must be strengthened before cleansing can take place. Dandelion[PP] builds strength in the liver.

CLEANSE: Unpleasant items such as heavy metals from the environment, mucus, and metabolic waste must be cleansed from all parts of the body in order to be healthy. Butcher's broom[PP] has been used to "sweep clean" any buildup in the circulatory system.

what parts are used?

The most effective parts of the plants or trees depend on the specific herb. Leaves, fruit, root, flowers, or bark can be used. For example, only the berries of the hawthorn[PP] plant are used for remedial purposes. Only the root is used in ginger[PP].

culinary herbs

When the word herb is used, you may think of culinary herbs, the delights of the cooking world that season our food. Although many of the herbs mentioned in this book are used in the kitchen, we'll only address the therapeutic uses of each herb.

So even though you'll see parsley[PP] in the chapter on Power Plants, it is not being referred to for its culinary uses.

final thoughts

You may remember, herbs were the special foods used by your grandmothers and grandfathers to support the body's natural healing processes. Unfortunately, we've lost that very basic focus on prevention and healing. We can learn from other cultures around the world that have regained a natural approach to health, or never lost it along the way. Japan, for example, eats kelp in many forms, usually as part of their daily diet. Americans (with our cultural bias) seldom think of kelp as food, but will consider it as a supplement. Remember, herbs are food—*nutrient-rich* food.

choosing herbs

herbs used to be scarce in the marketplace, making it necessary to seek out rare herb shops or health food stores. Now you can easily find herbs in drug stores and in the grocery store and even through the mail. This newfound popularity is good news. Herbal abundance is a sign of greater acceptance by the American public. The only bad news is that now you have to figure out which ones are pure, safe, and highest in quality. Like any food, lots of variables go into how well any crop grows and what nutrients result in the end product. Some of those variables are detailed below.

strain

Just like there are lots of strains of peas, there are many different strains of valerian[PP] (approximately two hundred). And some strains are more therapeutic than others.

growing conditions

The type of soil, air, and ground temperature, the amount and purity of precipitation and nutrients are all factors that determine how well an herb will work. Organic growing methods, for example, mean not only a lack of poisonous substances used, but also nutrient-enhancing practices like crop rotation.

time of harvest

The month of harvest, as well as the age of the plant at harvest, are both important. Ginseng[PP], for example, should only be harvested after the plant is eight years old to get the highest level of nutrients (like ginsenosides).

part of the plant used

Flowers, berries, barks, roots, stems, leaves, seeds or twigs can all be used, but not with equal effectiveness. For example, bilberry[PP] fruit has been used for vision and urinary tract infections. Use the leaves and you're wasting your time.

processing methods

Real expertise and experience are needed in the area of herb processing. Most food/herb processing destroys nutrients. Heat, for example, will destroy enzymes in the plant, making it harder to digest and absorb. Fillers or additives such as sugar or chemicals like artificial flavors and colors are common.

a note on "wildcrafting"

Picking your own fruit from the tree or vine is great when it comes to apples and strawberries or other "domestic" fruits and vegetables. But picking your own herbs from "the wild" should be limited to true experts in herbal botany. About one percent of all plants are highly poisonous. Some lethal plants look like innocent health-giving herbs. Simply put, don't risk your life.

final thoughts

Don't have time to pick up a quick Ph.D. in herbal agriculture so you can grow and harvest the most effective herbs? Without that degree, it's best to rely on a company that does their own pharmaceutical-quality testing of every batch of herbs which ensures that regardless of where in the world that batch originates, it will be pure and effective. Testing should include thorough chemical analysis to verify what is and is not in that capsule, extract, or tea. Knowledgeable herb shop or health food store personnel should be glad to share quality control documentation provided by herb companies.

food for thought

Do you have the quality control information that you need to know in regard to the herbal supplements you take? Wouldn't it be nice to have quality control assurances for all the food we eat?

herbs vs. drugs

physical and chemical differences

according to Webster's Dictionary, the definition of a drug is "any substance intended for use in the treatment or prevention of disease; any non-food substance intended to affect the structure or function of the body."[1] Food (specifically herbs) affects the structure and function of the body because of the nutrients that are contained in them. The difference is that food is not sold for the cure, prevention, and treatment or mitigation of disease. There are other very important differences between herbs and drugs. Let's look at some of them.

origin

Herbs, like any food, are made up of many different chemicals. Just as there is no patent on turnips, there are no patents on herbs. If a chemical is isolated from that herb, however, it can be patented and marketed as a drug. As a result, you have a drug that is a controlled substance because it no longer has the other buffers that make it safe as a food. A drug also no longer has the balance of nutrients (like vitamins, minerals, enzymes, fiber, and chlorophyll) that allow each other to work better. For example, our bodies can fully utilize calcium only when magnesium is present.

23

synthetics

Nearly eighty percent of all drugs on the market today are chemically modified or purified versions of substances found originally in plants.[2]

FOOTNOTES

1. *Webster's Universal College Dictionary*, 1997.
2. Louise Tenney, M.H., *The Encyclopedia of Natural Remedies*, p. 1.

mindset differences

"Every nectar is poison if taken in excess."
Hindu Proverb

to a certain degree, modern medicine has programmed Americans to look for the "quick fix." We often have the "it's-broken-just-fix-it" attitude, as if we were machines. It's not that simple. Herbs are not a substitute for drugs. Different choices that we make day to day regarding food, attitude, and lifestyle cause an overload of waste and toxins to build up in our cells until symptoms crop up. Those problems don't happen overnight and they can't be fixed overnight. Symptoms can be masked or suppressed by drugs without strengthening the body. If the real cause is not addressed, the problem will always surface later.

indoctrination

Many Americans have been indoctrinated with a quick fix drug mindset. One third of all commercials are drug advertisements. The average eighteen year old has been exposed to twenty thousand hours of glitzy, persuasive drug commercials![1] Eager to cash in on relaxed FDA regulations, drug manufacturers spent $277 milllion advertising prescription drugs on television in the first nine months of 1997.[2] Luckily, we have the option, however, to seek other opinions and make informed decisions.

overdosing

Overdosing is a legitimate fear when taking drugs. More than two hundred thousand deaths annually are attributed to adverse reactions to drugs.[3] But fatal reactions to herbs are virtually non-existent. That is not to say that we should not use caution when using herbs; they can be very powerful and should be treated with respect. More is not always better. And just as there can be an allergy to cantaloupe or something like oatmeal, there can be an allergy to an herb.

symptoms vs. cause

Americans have been conditioned to suppress symptoms, like using a cough suppressant to relieve a hacking cough. When using herbs, though, the approach to a cough is to work with the body to allow it to expel the mucus, not hold it in the body. When you fully understand healthy body processes, you can better cooperate and help the processes that heal the body.

example of symptom suppression

You have a bad cold with a low grade fever. The doctor says a cold is the result of a virus, and nothing can be done except to treat the symptoms. In an attempt to survive the workday, you take aspirin for the fever and aches, a cough suppressant, and something to dry up the Niagara Falls drip coming from your nose. Since the body uses fever to kill a virus, the aspirin is actually prolonging the natural recovery process. And since the body uses sinus drip and cough as a way to also rid the body of this viral invader, the cough suppressant and the decongestant are working against the body's attempt to heal itself. One study done at Johns Hopkins School of Hygeine and Health found that patients who used aspirin for colds had a weaker immune response to the infection and had fewer antibodies to fight the virus.[4] NOTE: Consult your health care professional when fever is high or unexplainable.

self-limiting illness

According to the *New England Journal of Medicine*, about ninety percent of the people who visit doctors have conditions that will either improve on their own (self-limited), or are beyond the reach of modern medicine to solve.[5] So if you let your body heal itself without outside interference, it will. In general, all your body requires in self-limiting illness (like a cold) is common sense approaches like rest, proper nutrition, and drinking lots of water. But we have been conditioned to believe that we need to take drugs to suppress symptoms of sickness. Work with a qualified health professional for guidance in this area.

taking pills

Many of us see pills as medicine. And with dehydrated herbs in capsules, you often run into a lot of pills to take in one day. We're often indoctrinated with the one-pill-a-day mindset and when faced with swallowing several herbal capsules, you feel overwhelmed. Don't be. Keep in mind that a dehydrated food will be bulkier. It is not a concentrated drug with all its side effects. The results will be well worth "all those pills." And if you aren't looking forward to swallowing a variety of pills, herbs can be ingested in several other forms.

final thoughts

The body works best when we support the natural processes that it knows are ideal for our health. Herbs can be taken to support the natural processes during illness. But more importantly, herbs can be used to keep you healthy so that you are less vulnerable to illness.

FURTHER READING

How To Get Well, by Paavo O. Airola, N.D., Ph.D., Health Plus, 1995.

FOOTNOTES

1. *Health News and Views,* The Life Connection (October 1996).
2. "Drug Ads Boost Sales and Doctors are Angry," *Associated Press/Daily News* (January 7, 1998) p. 1A.
3. Rick Ansorge, "Living Long," *Daily News/Freedom News Service* (September 8, 1996) p. C1.
4. Donna Alvarado, "Researchers say aspirin can make a cold worse," *Detroit Free Press/Knight Ridder Newspapers* (January 15, 1991) p. 4D.
5. *New England Journal of Medicine* (December 25, 1980).

differences in effect

S ymptoms have a bad reputation. Some symptoms are slight, some are significant. Either way, they are the body's way of giving us a flashing light signal to provide help or support in some way. If we saw a red flashing light on the dashboard of the car that said "check engine," would we suppress that signal by putting tape over it? The same is true with our body's signals.

symptoms vs. cause

Virtually all drugs treat symptoms, herbs address the root cause of a problem. For example, to "cure" constipation, chemical laxatives irritate the lining of the intestines. This irritation results in the body sending out warning signals to start immediate muscular contractions to expel the irritant—basically, a bowel movement begins. A natural approach to intestinal health is to provide the many different types of fiber that cause healthy bowel movements without irritation or discomfort.

side effects

According to *The American Medical Association Guide to Prescription and Over-The-Counter Drugs*, "all drugs have side effects."[1] If reading the contraindications and warnings on drug labels and inserts doesn't scare you, nothing will. Drugs are frequently being taken off the market due to problems with serious side effects. The reason that side effects occur is that drugs push symptoms back into the body. Unfortunately, since the cause of the problem has not been addressed, it will resurface. It's like using a pesticide in only one room of the house to kill bugs. They'll just migrate to another room or escape into the walls, only to reappear later. Like any food, herbs can occasionally cause an allergic reaction like a rash. If that occurs, discontinue use immediately. Sometimes herbs can cause slight stomach upset even when taken according to package recommendations. If that occurs, your body may be telling you that you're taking too much or that you don't need those nutrients at all.

example of masking symptoms

Here's a common example of masking symptoms without addressing the cause:

- ◆ You get frequent colds and use antihistamines and cough suppressants.
- ◆ Later you develop sinus infections and take antibiotics.
- ◆ The sinus infections keep coming back and one infection actually goes into pneumonia. Even with antibiotics, the pneumonia is hard to shake off.

Does this kind of progression sound familiar? Infection was "pushed" back into the tissues, only to resurface later.

reaction time

When you take herbs, you sometimes see results very quickly. Sometimes you need lots of patience to see a difference. An infinite number of factors come into play here. If you've had a problem for twenty years, you can't eliminate it in one day. And as all parents know, children's bodies tend to recover from illness very quickly compared to an adult. For more information, see the chapter on The Laws of Nature.

effectiveness comparison

Here's an example of the difference in saw palmetto[PP] (an herb often used for prostate health) and Proscar, which is the standard medical treatment for an enlarged prostate. Keep in mind that not all herbs are as comparatively effective—some more, some less.

- Many studies show saw palmetto[PP] to be ninety percent effective in a period of approximately four to six weeks. Proscar is effective in reducing symptoms in less than thirty-seven percent after one year.
- About five percent of the men taking Proscar will suffer from decreased libido, impotence, and other related disorders. There are no side effects with saw palmetto[PP].
- Proscar costs about $75 per month. Saw palmetto[PP] costs about $21 per month.

ADDITIONAL RESOURCES
Michael T. Murray, N.D., "Saw Palmetto: Nature's Answer To Enlarged Prostate", *Health Counselor Magazine* (reprint).

drug interactions

Medications often have serious adverse reactions when combined with other medications. The National Institute for Drug Abuse estimates that one million Americans who suffer from adverse drug reactions and harmful combinations have been misdiagnosed as senile.[2]

no drugs?

There is a time and place for drugs and surgery. In an emergency situation like a serious car accident or acute infections, surgery or drugs may be the only alternatives. If you avoid prescription and over-the-counter drugs for the day to day problems of life, you'll find that drugs will work much better if they are needed. Frequent use of antibiotics, for example, often causes a resistance to all antibiotics as the body adapts to the drugs.

saying "no" to drugs?

Never discontinue the use of a prescription without consulting a qualified health professional. Many drugs are critical to sustaining life. Some drugs will cause dangerous withdrawal symptoms when discontinued abruptly. Even some over-the-counter medications can cause withdrawal symptoms when discontinued abruptly.

normalize?

Herbs tend to "normalize" or balance body processes. In contrast, drugs are highly specialized and "force" the body into compliance. There are drugs, for example, that lower blood pressure and there are drugs that raise blood pressure. On the other hand, herbs for blood pressure tend to support the body's processes so that blood pressure is normalized whether it started out too high or too low.

FOOTNOTES

1. *The American Medical Association Guide to Prescription and Over-The-Counter Drugs*, p. 26.
2. Louise Tenney, *Nutritional Guide with Food Combining*, p. 48.

financial differences

"Nothing is more fatal to health than an overcare of it."
Benjamin Franklin

i t is impossible to put a price tag on achieving optimal wellness. But budgetary restrictions and common sense force you to take a serious look into the financial differences of using herbs and drugs.

pricing

"Prescription drug prices rose three times faster than inflation in the last decade [sic 1983–1993], making the drug industry the nation's most profitable business."[1] In general, drugs are considerably more expensive than herbs. According to the National Association of Chain Drugstores, the average wholesale cost of the top seven prescribed drugs in 1991 was $45.08.[2] The wholesale cost of the highest quality single herbs averaged $6.45.

prevention

A growing number of Americans are realizing the value of the adage "a stitch in time saves nine." If we strengthen the body and its systems (like the immune system) through nutrition, we can avoid or considerably delay the need for drugs and even surgeries. Even if the quality of life were not a factor, avoiding surgery that costs over $100,000 (not an uncommon price for a surgical procedure) is worth a great deal.

insurance

The vast majority of insurance policies do not currently cover herbs or other preventive health measures. A growing number of companies, however, are finally realizing the financial value of prevention and are making changes. Be proactive. Let your insurance company know your opinion on this subject. Insurance companies need to know what their customers think, whether you believe preventive health should or should not be covered.

final thoughts

Making the right decisions in regard to your health is not an easy task. Hopefully the facts presented in this section have helped you come to a conclusion that is right for your body.

food for thought

How much would you spend for a cure if you were faced with a terminal illness? How much would you spend to prevent that illness?

FURTHER READING

Making Medicine, Making Money by Donald Drake and Marian Uhlman, Universal Press Syndicate, 1993.
Health and Healing by Andrew Weil, M.D., Houghton Mifflin, 1995.
Modern Day Plagues by Louise Tenney, M.H., Woodland, 1994.

FOOTNOTES

1. Donald Drake and Marian Uhlman, *Making Medicine, Making Money*, cover, © 1993.
2. IBID., p.60.

taking herbs

who needs herbs?

"Faced with the choice between changing one's mind and proving there is no need to do so, almost everybody gets busy on the proof."
John Kenneth Galbraith

Our soils are depleted of nutrients. A recent study at Rutgers University reported that today's chemically grown produce has eighty-seven percent fewer nutrients.[1] Refined foods lose nutrients like minerals, essential fatty acids, and vitamins B, C, and E. The fast pace of current life, a poor diet, and toxins in our environment cause tremendous stress on our bodies. We also inherit certain strengths and weaknesses from our ancestors. So do virtually all Americans need supplements? Probably. A few groups stand out in the need for herbal supplements and are outlined below.

children

It's critical for growing bones, muscles, nerves, and other tissues to have optimal nutrition. Would you build a house with inferior materials and expect a structure that can stand up to the elements? Then why build a body with inferior material like processed, lifeless junk food (pseudofood)? The early, formative years are critical to developing healthy eating habits and building a structure to last a lifetime. Herbs can play an essential role in childhood nutrition. According to the National Center for Health Statistics, there were 47,787,000 prescriptions for antibiotics for American children under the age of sixteen in 1995. The leading prescription for Attention Deficit Hyperactivity Disorder (ADHD), Ritalin, is used daily by more than 1.5 million American children under nineteen years of age.[2] Many people are unaware that there are natural alternatives.

FURTHER READING

The ABC Herbal, by Steven H. Horne, Wendell W. Whitman Co., 1992.
Feingold Cookbook for Hyperactive Children, by Ben Feingold, M.D. and Helene Feingold, Random House, 1979.

seniors ──────────

Unfortunately, we sometimes get less active and don't pay as much attention to balanced nutrition as we age. The accumulation of waste in the tissues also takes its toll over the years, resulting in illness. Many seniors have a long list of health problems with a corresponding long list of prescriptions and side effects. Experts say twenty-five percent of Americans aged sixty-five or older may suffer from malnutrition.[3] Herbs can help to bridge the nutritional gap.

pregnant women ──────────

Studies on the impact of folic acid on neural tube defects (like Spina Bifida) have shown how important nutrition is before conception. We are only beginning to find out the impact of other nutrients on the unborn. (For more information about using herbs during pregnancy, refer to the chapter on Power Plants or the index. Remember to always consult with a qualified health professional before adding a supplement to your diet during pregnancy.)

FURTHER READING

Herbal Healing For Women by Rosemary Gladstar, Simon and Schuster, 1993.

Today's Herbal Health for Women by Louise Tenney, M.H. and Deborah Lee, Woodland, 1996.

The Woman's Encyclopedia of Natural Healing by Dr. Gary Null, Seven Stories Press, 1996.

athletes and those who exercise

Athletes have special needs when it comes to nutrition whether you're a serious weightlifter or you simply work out at the gym when you get the chance. Stamina and a body that is strong enough to resist injury· are both important to the athlete. Perspiration can also result in the loss of electrolyte minerals (calcium, magnesium, sodium, potassium, and chloride). Building muscle requires a protein that is easily digested and used by the body. Herbs can be a great source for these nutrients.

pets

Yes, even pets can benefit from herbs. Garlic[PP], for example, has been used for flea control and infections. Liquids, oils, ointments, and creams are the most easy to use. But even capsules or tablets can be added to their diet. Homeopathics are also a good choice for making pets healthy and happy.

FURTHER READING

Natural Health for Dogs and Cats by Richard H. Pitcairn, D.V.M., Ph.D. and Susan Hubble Pitcairn, Rodale Press, 1995.

RDA shortfalls

Extensive surveys of the American diet show that ninety-two percent of us don't even get the Recommended Dietary Allowance (RDA) of essential nutrients.[4] The RDA is established as the level at which the specific disease for that deficiency would not occur. The RDA for vitamin C, for example, is the level at which you're probably safe from scurvy. Optimum health levels are substantially higher.

reality check

Do you have more than enough physical, mental and emotional energy to accomplish anything you'd like to do? Do you have more than enough energy without the use of artificial substances like caffeine, sugar, alcohol, tobacco, or other drugs that put stress on your body?

final thoughts

If you eat nothing but organically grown food, have a stress-free existence, live far away from concentrations of toxins in our air, water, and earth, and have inherited a great set of genes, consider yourself very blessed—you're one of a kind. The rest of us need supplements.

FURTHER READING

Empty Harvest by Dr. Bernard Jensen and Mark Anderson,
  Avery Publishing, 1990.

FOOTNOTES

1. Lee M. Schwalben, M.D., "When Eating Healthy Just Isn't Enough," *Healthy and Natural Journal*, 4, I 3, p.66.
2. Earl Ubell, "Are Our Children Overmedicated?" *Parade Magazine* (October 12, 1997) p. 4-6.
3. Cassandra Burrell, "Elderly Often Don't Eat Well," *Daily News (Associated Press)* p.C1 (June 10, 1997).
4. Patrick Quillin, Ph.D., R.D., C.N.S., *Healing Secrets from the Bible*, p. 83.

herbal preparations

different forms of herbs are effective for different needs. If you find yourself facing a grab bag selection of herbal preparations without a clue about which forms are the best choice for you, here are some definitions to help you with your choices.

capsules and tablets

Capsules and tablets are a very popular way to take herbs. They are convenient to take and are precisely measured. With capsules and tablets you can also avoid strong or unpleasant tastes. Vegetarians sometimes prefer tablets since capsules are made with gelatin. If you're taking tablets, special care must be taken to select tablets from companies that have not used processing methods that destroy nutrients.

decoction

To "decoct" an herb means to boil it for five to twenty minutes. Roots, twigs, and barks are boiled to extract the substances that

41

don't fully dissolve in hot water like they would in a tea. Decoction allows the essential mineral salts and alkaloids to be extracted but destroys beneficial volatile oils (oils that are destroyed at high temperatures).

dried herbs

Dried herbs are sold in bulk and are usually used as a tea (also called an infusion). They can also be put into capsules.

essential oils

Aromatherapy and personal care products such as perfumes, skin treatments, bath oils, and massage oils use essential (volatile) oils that have been extracted from herbs. Tea tree oil[PP] is an essential oil and is used as a first aid product. These oils are almost always used externally and usually have a strong aroma.

extracts and tinctures

Herbs are usually soaked in an alcohol solution and strained when preparing extracts and tinctures. This form of herb is concentrated and especially useful for children, pets, and seniors who may have trouble swallowing pills. This concentrated form of herb is also helpful for external use, like valerian[PP] for a sprain. The alcohol is merely used as a preservative. If you want to avoid the alcohol, put the number of drops to be used at one time in a spoon and allow the alcohol to evaporate (about twenty-five minutes). Some products are alcohol-free and contain glycerine as a preservative. Extracts and tinctures are different from homeopathics. Extracts and tinctures are often added to natural cosmetics and cleansing products like shampoo.

ointments and creams

Herbs that are commonly used on the skin are often formulated in salves and creams for convenience and prolonged exposure to the skin.

powders (bulk)

Some herbs are ground into a fine powder for easy mixing with juice or water. Many of the green juices (like barley juice) and fiber products (like psyllium) are sold in this form. Powders can also be made into a paste by adding water and applied externally. A paste of activated charcoal[PP], for example, can be applied to insect bites.

making teas (infusions)

To brew tea, place a heaping tablespoon of dried herbs into a cup of hot water. Let the mixture steep for ten minutes, strain, and drink. Teas can be made in advance but must be refrigerated. Two capsules can be added to a cup of boiling water, steeped ten minutes, strained, and used as a tea. A couple of encounters with some therapeutic herbs in the form of tea lets you know why capsules and tablets are popular. Some of them have a pleasant taste, like licorice and chamomile[PP], but others like goldenseal[PP] and valerian[PP] may make you beg for mercy!

final thoughts

Choose the way you get your herbs based on convenience, whether you need to use them externally or internally, and your own personal preference. The best of herbal intentions won't benefit anyone if supplements remain in the cupboard unused.

taking herbs 101

taking herbs can be as confusing as choosing how to ingest them. Listed below are a few things to keep in mind when you take herbs that will help you get the most out of the nutrients.

freshness

Like any food, freshness is important. Make sure all herbs are tightly capped and stored in dark bottles that keep light from deteriorating the nutrients. Keeping herbs in a cool place will also keep them from deteriorating. Some herbs specify refrigeration but it is important to remember that herbs will not last forever. Under ideal conditions, herbs last about three years.

medications

If taking prescriptions or over-the-counter drugs, take them at least an hour before or after taking your herbs. Many drugs are acidic and can weaken the effect of an herb. Drugs can impact the nutrients in any food, including herbs. Antacids can inhibit the absorption of phosphorous and aspirin can affect iron and folic acid levels.[1] Consult with a health care professional who is familiar with herbs to determine which herbs can be taken while using certain medications.

water, water, everywhere

Make sure you take capsules and tablets with pure water to rehydrate them so that the body can absorb them. For more information on appropriate amounts, see the chapter on Water Works: The Uninary System.

with meals

Since nutrients tend to work better in the presence of other specific nutrients, take herbs with food. For example, the body needs vitamin C to digest iron. Exceptions to this general rule should be labeled "take between meals." It's best to take herbs immediately before meals. Delay between the herbs and the rest of your meal can occasionally result in slight stomach upset since some herbs are very strong. The herbs will be digested better and faster if taken first. Anyone with serious digestive problems, such as ulcers, should exercise special caution.

chewing?

Chewing or "swishing" herbs (like any food) before swallowing can start the flow of enzymes. Enzymes allow the body to absorb the nutrients in herbs. Some herbs have a strong flavor and are not good candidates for chewing. Swishing may not add to your popularity at dinner parties but getting the enzymes started in the digestive process will help you to get more out of your herbs.

how much? ───────────

Reading the label is very important. Also, listen to your body. If you get a slight case of upset stomach or indigestion, cut back on the amount. It's best to work up to the full amount gradually, especially if you are in a weakened condition.

how much for children? ───────────

Here are some suggested guidelines to calculate the amount of herbs needed by children. Adjust accordingly for children who are especially small or large for their age.

Age	Dose
Babies	1/8
2 – 6 years	1/5
7 – 9 years	1/4
10 – 14 years	1/2
15 years and older	Full

memory aids ───────────

Do you have trouble remembering to take herbs or remembering whether you have actually taken them during the day? Many drug stores have handy plastic pill trays that have compartments marked "morning," "noon," etc. Plastic snack/sandwich bags with labels can also be used. If you take several supplements, the key is sorting them in advance and having them handy when you need them.

a word on labels ───────────

The Dietary Supplement Health and Education Act was a federal law passed in 1994 and allows manufacturers to list the known effects of herbal supplements. Most herb companies have been very conservative with health claims on labels in the past and it was often difficult to tell which herbs targeted which area of health. The FDA also established new regulations regarding labels in September 1997. "Supplement Facts" will be required on bottles of herbs and will include details on the part of the plant used (like roots or bark) and the solvents used in processing.[2] These new labels must appear within eighteen months (March 1999) of the FDA's ruling.

biochemical individuality

Biochemical individuality is a mouthful that just means every individual's body chemistry is very different from someone else's. For that reason our nutritional needs are all different. There are twenty-four different herbs that are effective in providing relief to an ailing urinary system. Which one is right for you?

selecting the right herb

The many available choices of herbs can be overwhelming when you first start taking herbs. Weeding out and selecting the right herb for your particular needs can keep you from wasting your money. The following are some rules of thumb in making your choices, in order of effectiveness.

- ◆ Alternative health professionals that use tools such as iridology and kinesiology can help you target the most effective choice (for more information, refer to the chapter "Other Natural Health Approaches").
- ◆ Reviewing the information in the chapter on Power Plants and the Systems Summary in the Appendix can help you select the herb that most fits your needs. Consider factors such as the body systems and specific problems for which the herbs have been historically used, whether infection exists, and whether you want to gently build before you cleanse.

- ◆ Selecting a combination herb targeted to the system of the body you'd like to strengthen can also be effective. To increase your chances for the most effective choice, review each individual herb in the combinations available for applicability to your needs.
- ◆ Alternating different herbs is also helpful. When your body has enough of the particular nutrients in a specific herb or combination, change your nutrients. Changing every three months can provide variety.

final thoughts

A holistic approach will always serve you well. If, for example, you'd like to increase your energy levels, consider the following factors:

- ◆ Is the real problem that you're not able to get enough sleep? Exercise, schedule changes, or an herb such as hops to help you sleep may be the answer.
- ◆ Is the real problem that you are under a lot of stress? An herb like valerian[PP] or chamomile[PP] to help your stress levels could be the answer.
- ◆ Energy levels are also impacted by imbalances in blood sugar and the thyroid. A visit to your health professional may be appropriate.

In any case, take the time to think through the possibilities and analyze your situation like you peel an onion—one layer at a time.

FOOTNOTES

1. *The Columbia Encyclopedia of Nutrition*, Ed. Myron Winick, M.D., p. 128.
2. "Washington Update", *Energy Times* (November/December 1997) p. 72.

what to expect

the laws of nature

*"We squander health to gain wealth; as we get older,
we squander wealth in search of health."*
Freia Eady

if you want to work with the body, it helps to understand how the body works, and in particular, how it heals itself. Don't worry. You're not going to get a lesson in biophysics and biochemistry. The principles are very basic.

dr. ritchason

Dr. Jack Ritchason is a naturopathic doctor and well-respected author. The two rules of thumb outlined below are from his "Golden Rules of Health."

- It takes five to seven times the nutrition to build and repair than it takes to maintain.
- Nothing heals in the human body in less than three months; then add one month for every year that you have been sick.

Using the second rule, if you've had ear infections for three years, you can expect to take herbs for that area of the body for about six months. Keep in mind that the best rule is only a rough estimate.

reaction time

Sometimes you see results quickly when you take herbs. Sometimes it takes longer. Some individuals respond better to herbs than others due to factors such as dietary habits and how strong a constitution that person has. The most effective herb won't work if it's still in the bottle. You may see improvement in symptoms quickly. Long-term benefits like increased energy may take longer. With an inherited weakness, you may need to take a maintenance dosage of herbs for long periods of time.

the healing cleanse

*"For every disease that afflicts mankind, there is a treatment
or a cure occurring naturally on this earth."*
Dr. Norman Farnsworth, Pharmacologist, University of Illinois

When you feed your body the nutrition it needs, your cells respond and begin to rid themselves of waste more easily. Occasionally, however, the body overreacts to an infusion of nutrients and begins eliminating waste in a panicky discharge of poisons and toxins. This process is called a "healing cleanse." Such a cleanse can be good and bad news: the good news is that your body is in good enough health to get rid of toxic waste buildup. The bad news is that your affected tissues are getting rid of waste and toxins so quickly that your body can't remove the debris fast enough and it lingers in the body.

rushing it

If you begin too many herbs at once, the mechanisms in the body that eliminate waste may be overloaded too quickly with debris. The same principle holds true of any abrupt change to a healthier lifestyle. If you change eating or exercise habits too quickly, a healing cleanse (also known as a healing crisis) can occur. Let's look at it this way: even the most efficient waste management company is overwhelmed when given too much garbage to handle at one time. Even the healthiest of approaches can be too much of a shock to the body. Walking five miles a day is great, but if you try five miles the first day of your exercise program, you will be sorry. Our bodies respond much better to a gradual approach. This doesn't mean that you can't start more than one herb at a time, but it is a warning of the complications that may arise when doing so.

recognizing a healing cleanse

The following signs are typical during a healing cleanse:

- Feeling "off the mark" immediately after a phase of feeling great
- Burning or cloudy urine
- Burning, loose stools
- Sinus or chest congestion
- Skin eruptions, rashes or extremely dry or oily skin
- A metallic or medicinal taste in the mouth (from medicines that were previously taken)
- A coating on the tongue
- Strong body odor

Your body will generally go through illnesses that have been experienced in the past, in reverse order. This is especially true if medications were used to suppress symptoms in the past. You will generally feel the symptoms without really feeling "sick."

example of a healing cleanse

In the past, you have suffered with recurrent bladder infections. You begin taking corn silk, parsley[PP], and uva ursi[PP] to strengthen the urinary tract. You begin taking them at the same time and immediately take the full amount specified on each bottle. Three weeks later you begin to feel burning when you urinate and notice the urine is cloudy. The next day your bowel movements are loose and burning. You feel uncomfortable, but not sick like you did when you had the bladder infection and took the antibiotics.

caution

When going through a healing cleanse, it's often difficult to determine whether it is a cleanse or illness. Always work with a qualified health care professional to determine which is the case. In the case of the urinary tract example above, an infection can be dangerous if left untreated.

minimizing the opportunity

The best way to avoid a drastic healing cleanse is to make a gradual transition to a healthier you:

- Build up to dosages gradually.
- Gradually add herbs to your program. Adding one herb at a time also may let you know which ones are more effective than others.
- Limit the number of different herbs that you take.
- Make sure that all your elimination channels are working well before you start taking herbs or adding herbs to your program!

elimination channels

No, this has nothing to do with a violent channel on cable television. The elimination channels are the means by which your body gets rid of waste generated during normal body processes and toxins accumulated from the environment (like chemicals in the water and air). The major elimination channels are:

- The urinary system
- The intestinal system
- The respiratory system
- The skin

By making sure these pathways are clear, you can prevent a minor or major "clog" from happening. Open channels ensure open escape routes for the waste and toxins being "stirred up." The chapters that follow will give some ideas on how to provide a little assurance that your "exits" are open.

what if?

If a healing cleanse strikes despite your attempts to prevent it, here are some ideas you may want to try for a few days to speed up the exit of all that stuff you're trying so diligently to eliminate.

- Drink at least eight glasses of pure water each day. If you're drinking less than that amount, work up to that level gradually.
- Minimize or eliminate eating (however, special caution should be taken while fasting). A fresh juice fast for a few days, for example, allows the energy that would have been used for digesting to be used for healing. If you eat, concentrate on fresh fruit and vegetables. When you're not feeling well, a lack of appetite is often a good indicator from your body that it needs a rest from digestion.
- Get lots of rest. You'll be tired because your body is diverting precious energies to healing your ailments. Let your body take an emotional and physical rest so it can clean house.
- Brisk, dry skin brushing gets the dead layer of skin cells off so that your skin can breathe and eliminate acidic waste. The lymphatic and circulatory systems also benefit. For more details, see the chapter "Other Natural Health Approaches."

- Soak in a hot bath with ginger[PP], sage, and bentonite clay. About six capsules each of ginger and sage open the pores and bentonite clay (about a cup of hydrated or 1/2 cup of dry) draws out toxins.
- Double the amount of herbs you have been taking for the area that you are cleansing. EXAMPLE: In the example of the urinary cleanse previously mentioned, you would double the amount of corn silk, parsley[PP], and uva ursi[PP] you've been taking. The stress on your body will use up more vitamins and minerals during a cleanse. Potassium and vitamin C are especially important.
- Using enemas or colonics. All those grandmothers were right. When you're not feeling well, getting those toxins out of there can really help.
- For more details in each of these areas, see the following chapters on elimination channels. If properly supported, a cleanse should only last a few days.

healing signs

Over the long haul, there are signs to look for that will tell you that your health is improving. The signs may be obvious, like increased energy or feeling less "stressed out." Or the signs may be less obvious. Your hair may get thicker and look healthier. If you're taking calcium-rich herbs like horsetail or slippery elm[PP], you may develop moons on your fingernails where there were none. Look for the signs along the way when you take herbs, but in particular, after a healing cleanse is over. For more information on what to look for, read the next chapter "Signs of the Times."

final thoughts

Going through a healing cleanse is not fun, but it is a sign of progress. Be gradual in your program: this can help you avoid a healing cleanse. But if one strikes, support it to speed the exit of the cellular debris that has been "stirred up."

food for thought

- ◆ Have you had a recent physical?
- ◆ How sure are you that all your elimination channels are in great working order?
- ◆ What areas might need special attention and what ideas would you like to try?

    The uninary system? _____

    _____

    The intestinal system? _____

    _____

    The respiratory system? _____

    _____

    The skin? _____

    _____

FURTHER READING

The Encyclopedia of Natural Remedies by Louise Tenney, M.H., Woodland, 1995.

Doctor-Patient Handbook by Bernard Jensen, D.C., Nutritionist, Bernard Jensen Enterprises, 1976.

signs of the times

a red octagonal sign—we know it means "stop" without reading the words. What about our health? Are there obvious signs that tell us when things are going sour? You can count on it. We can choose to listen or we can choose to ignore. Do we wake up one day with a health crisis or does it take years to build up to the point we can't "ignore it and hope it goes away?" It doesn't happen overnight. So what are the signs along the way? Over the years, as we eat some things we shouldn't and fail to eat some things we should, waste builds up in our tissues. Other contributing factors are the things in our environment that also accumulate in our bodies like chemicals in our water and air. These problems settle in the tissues of our bodies based on our inherited weaknesses. So if you inherited the genes that mean your Achilles' heel is your lungs, you may end up with chronic bronchitis, asthma, or respiratory allergies.

what are some of the signs?

Some are more obvious than others, like pain, swelling, changes in body functions (like a difference in bowel movements), or a

59

change in the appearance of a mole. These signals are the body's way of sending out a distress signal and should be checked by your doctor as soon as possible. But there are other indicators that we need to heed if we want to maintain good health. Also watch these signs for indicators of improved health when you start taking herbs. They are a good way to confirm that you're on the right track to improved health. Some of them are listed below.

fingernails & toenails

A lack of moons (that white half circle) on each nail indicates you may not be eating or absorbing enough calcium. Sometimes a hydrochloric acid deficiency or thyroid imbalance exists. Thick, opaque nails can indicate a circulatory or thyroid problem. Ridges can mean poor nutrient absorption, stress, kidney problems, or arthritis. Nails that chip, peel, or crack easily can indicate a mineral, protein, or hydrochloric acid deficiency. White spots can indicate a zinc or thyroid deficiency. A purple or blue cast to the nail beds can mean a circulatory or respiratory problem. Flat nails often indicate Raynaud's disease. Yellow nails can be an indication of diabetes, respiratory or liver disorders, and vitamin E deficiency.

skin

Rough, dry, flaky skin can also be a sign of a mineral or thyroid imbalance or a lack of essential fatty acids in your diet.

hair

Is it thinning out? Dry? Brittle? Prematurely gray? Lifeless? If an overabundance of color and curl chemicals are not the culprit, it may be your diet. A lack of minerals or protein or a thyroid imbalance can sometimes be the reason for a problem.

final thoughts

The best rule of thumb is to watch out for the road signs, have your doctor check any unusual signs, and feed your "vehicle" the right nutrients to keep on going . . . and going . . . and going. And look for those road signs that let you know you're on the next higher rung of the ladder to better health.

FURTHER READING

Prescription for Nutritional Healing, James F. Balch, M.D., Phyllis H. Balch, C.N.C., Avery, 1997.

Healthy Healing, Linda Rector Page, N.D., Ph.D., 10th edition, Healthy Healing Publications, 1996.

food for thought

What are the signs I see when I look at my...

FINGERNAILS/TOENAILS:

       COLOR?_____

       SHAPE?_____

       THICKNESS?_____

       MOONS?_____

       SPOTS?_____

   SKIN:_____

   HAIR:_____

major
elimination
channels

overview

"...they might see with their eyes, hear with their ears, understand with their hearts, and turn and be healed."
Isaiah 6:10 NIV

elimination of waste from the body is usually not a popular dinner party topic of conversation. Elimination is messy, unpleasant—and underappreciated. We generally take the body's daily processes for granted until something goes wrong, like constipation, a cold, or a bladder infection. A holistic, preventive approach looks at what can be done before trouble brews with your elimination channels. So when you use herbs to build a healthier "you," you ensure that you open up those exits so that the potential discomforts of a healing cleanse can be avoided.

getting started

The best place to start is the urinary system, but making sure your intestines, respiratory system, and skin are all doing their respective jobs is also important. Think of the elimination channels as several rivers off of a lake. When any of the rivers gets dammed up, it puts extra pressure and dangerous levels of water in the lake and remaining rivers. That's the way our bodies work. If we "clog up" the urinary system, it can't handle its fair share of the load and as a result, the other channels are overworked and burdened.

what's next?

The following chapters outline some tips on how to make sure your "rivers" don't get dammed up. Some are obvious. Some may surprise you. For more information on individual herbs that can help each of the elimination channels, see the Appendix. For information on specific problems, like diarrhea, check the index.

water works:
the urinary system

the urinary system plays a crucial role in the evacuation of waste from the body. Unfortunately, it is also one of the most delicate systems in the body and is readily prone to infection and disease. Every person must fortify and protect the urinary system—and when infection occurs, swift and thorough action must be taken.

the mechanics

The kidney, bladder, ureters, and urethra make up the urinary tract. The urinary system is our waste water treatment plant and is crucial to our overall health. The urinary system removes waste from normal body processes, toxins, excess water, and excess ions from the bloodstream.

when trouble brews

When we overload and overstress the urinary system with normal waste products, toxins, or acidity, we will eventually pay the price. Results may be infections, high blood pressure, incontinence, kidney stones or even potentially fatal kidney failure. This overload may be due to an inherited weakness, structural problems (like damage from an accident), dietary indiscretions, or overloading the other elimination channels.

the offenders

The following items are some of the major stresses that can overload the urinary system:

- Not drinking enough water.
- Drinking colas and coffee.
- Drinking excess alcohol (more than the equivalent of a beer, a six ounce glass of wine, or a mixed drink with one ounce of alcohol daily).
- Eating excesses of protein (especially meat and milk).
- Consuming an excessive amount of salt.
- Taking non-steroidal anti-inflammatories like Tylenol®, and Advil®. According to the *New England Journal of Medicine*, one acetominophen every four days increases the chance of kidney disease 2.4 times; one ibuprofen, 8.8 times.[1]
- Eating an excessive amount of refined sugar and chocolate.
- Taking antibiotics (which can disrupt the normal balance of good and bad bacteria).
- Using birth control chemicals or a diaphragm.

action plan

Minimizing or eliminating the offenders listed above makes a big difference. Here are some clarifications and some additional ideas that may help.

- Drink eight glasses of pure water daily. The needs of a five-year-old will obviously be less that those of a linebacker. Jim Jenks, H.M.D., uses a very effective, easy system to calculate for calculating how much water you need daily in his book *Herb Power* . A half an ounce of water for every pound of body weight just means you divide your weight in half for the number of ounces you need. If you weigh one hundred pounds, you generally need about fifty ounces of water a day. Fresh vegetable and fruit juices and herbal teas can count toward that amount also. Minimize fruit juices and sweeteners in the herbal tea. For every glass of another type of beverage, add that same amount of water to the amount you need. Also add enough water to hydrate the herbs you take and to allow for excessive perspiration, if needed. If you don't drink enough water, gradually build up to this amount or you'll feel like you're going to explode or live in the bathroom!

- Drink *pure* water. Bottled water has not fared well under tests for purity (bacterial and chemical). Reverse osmosis and distilling are the most effective methods of making sure that water is purified.
- Drinking ten ounces of cranberry juice[pp] daily can be a preventive measure against infections.[2] Make sure you get a one hundred percent juice product that has no sugar.
- When you gotta' go, ya' gotta' go. Holding in urine will encourage the growth of bacteria and put unecessary stress on the bladder and prostate. In addition, straining and rushing when you urinate will add unneeded stress to the sphincter muscles.
- Eat a low-acid diet that avoids coffee, refined sugar, nonherbal teas, chocolate, alcohol, tomato products, and spicy foods.

water works herbs

Don't despair if you're not where you want to be with your action plan for urinary health. The following herbs have been used to feed the urinary tract and can help you with your plan. The herbs appearing in bold are most frequently used for the urinary system, but the others can be very helpful, as well. Look for combination herbs that have those herbs appearing in bold lettering for your best bet for the urinary system.

- **BILBERRY**[PP] is used for soothing the burning of urinary infections.
- BUCHU absorbs excess uric acid and is therefore used for kidney problems (like infections, urethritis, prostate* problems, bedwetting and cystitis).
- CHICKWEED is a soothing herb used for inflammation and infection.
- **CORNSILK** is used for kidney and bladder problems and bedwetting.
- COUCH GRASS is used for bladder infections and kidney problems.
- **CRANBERRY**[PP] is used for infections and kidney problems.
- DANDELION[PP] is used for strengthening the kidneys.
- HORSETAIL[PP] is used for bladder problems, kidney stones, urinary ulcers, and suppressed urination.
- **HYDRANGEA**[PP] is used for infections, kidney stones, and water retention.
- JUNIPER BERRY[PP] is used for kidney infections and water retention.
- LICORICE has been used to clear excess fluid and mucus from the body.
- MARSHMALLOW[PP] is a very soothing herb used for kidney problems and urinary bleeding. (The herb bears no resemblance to the jet-puffed variety)
- **PARSLEY**[PP] is used for bladder infections, fluid retention , and kidney inflammation.
- PEACH BARK is used for strengthening the bladder and alleviating water retention and mucus.
- SAW PALMETTO[PP] is commonly used for the prostate.*
- SCHIZANDRA is a strong immune system builder that is used for kidney problems.
- SIBERIAN GINSENG[PP] is a powerful tonic that can aid the urinary system.

- ◆ **SLIPPERY ELM**[PP] is another soothing herb used for kidney infections.
- ◆ **UVA URSI**[PP] is used for Bright's disease, prostate problems*, and infections.
- ◆ **YELLOW DOCK** is used for the bladder.

Herbs that are generally used for infections, such as goldenseal[PP], echinacea[PP], garlic, and Oregon grape[PP] are often used for urinary tract infections.

[PP] For more information on these herbs (including cautions), refer to the section on "Power Plants."

final thoughts

Neglecting the urinary system can have serious consequences. With a little care, the urinary system can become as healthy as a free-flowing mountain brook.

FOOTNOTES

1. *New England Journal of Medicine*, 331, No. 25(1994), p. 1675-8.
2. *The Journal of the American Medical Association* (March 9, 1994).

waste management: the intestines

"Cleanliness is next to Godliness."
Mothers everywhere

i ntestinal health is critical to your overall health. It is estimated that eighty percent of all diseases start in the large intestine.[1] The intestines are the body's sewage treatment plant and we all know what happens when the local sewage plant backs up: Bad news.

the mechanics

The large intestine and the rectum assume the responsibility for getting rid of undigested waste for the entire body. Undigested food passes from the small intestines as a liquid where most of the water and mineral salts are absorbed back into the body. The end product is:

- ◆ 60 - 70 percent water.
- ◆ 10 - 30 percent bacteria.
- ◆ Indigestible fiber.
- ◆ Dead cells and other waste materials.

Peristalsis is the progressive wave of muscular contraction that moves the food that you eat all the way through the body. When you eat, peristalsis begins to move your food. The muscular contractions also start in the intestines, causing a bowel movement. So if our digestive systems are working properly, every time we have a full meal, we should have a bowel movement. And each bowel movement should only take a couple of minutes. If you're a long way from that point, don't be discouraged. Read on for some tips to make "waste management" easier.

system overload

Since World War II, the typical American diet has suffered from a thirty-one percent increase in fats, a fifty percent increase in sugar and other sweeteners, and a forty-three percent decrease in complex carbohydrates like vegetables, whole grains, and beans.[2] If you're familiar with the computer term "garbage in, garbage out," you know that you can't expect good results when the input lacks integrity. The same principle applies with food. Don't expect a healthy body from inferior "fuel."

Read labels. If you can't pronounce the ingredients, chances are good that you're getting "pseudofood." Unfortunately, a high percentage of the American diet is not really food. Processed foods contain high levels of chemicals like preservatives, artificial flavors and colors, texturizers—and the list goes on and on. And what starts out as real food, like whole wheat flour, is "denatured". Nutrients are removed with chemicals so that you not only lose the goodness, you gain the chemical residue. High levels of sugar are added to processed food in an attempt put some flavor back, but you need a Ph.D. in sugar to tell what all the different names for sugar really mean. The more we concentrate on whole, natural foods, the more our bodies will thank us with improved health.

transit time

The ideal amount of time between eating and eliminating is twenty-four to thirty-six hours. Any longer than that period of time allows the food to ferment, resulting in autointoxication or self-poisoning. Fermentation causes toxic substances like phenols to be found in urine samples. The presence of toxins like phenols can lead to chronic problems like allergies, acne, and breast disease.[3] If you have any doubt about the toxic nature of the contents of your colon, think of a baby's diaper. Delays in removing soiled diapers will result in rashes or skin that is irritated and appears to be burnt.

probiotics

Probiotics means "for life." That is the term used for the good bacteria that helps digest food, creates vitamins like B12 and K, and inhibits the growth of disease-promoting bacteria or fungus such as yeast. *Lactobacillus acidophilus* and *bifidobacterium bifidum* are two common types. A diet rich in vegetables, whole grains, and legumes helps to promote the growth of these "good guys."

antibiotics

Antibiotics destroy the good bacteria with the bad, causing a weakened immune system and an overgrowth of yeast (*candida albicans*). The increased use of antibiotics in livestock feeds has prompted many Americans to become vegetarians. In the 1970s, Great Britain and the European Economic Community (EEC) banned the chronic use of antibiotics in livestock feed[4] (just another opportunity to learn from other countries!) Increased use of antibiotics (through our food as well as through the pharmacy) is also causing an increase in reports of antibiotic-resistant bacteria in the news. For natural alternatives to antibiotics, refer to Oregon grape[PP], garlic[PP], goldenseal[PP], echinacea[PP], and tea tree oil[PP] in the Power Plants chapter .

FURTHER READING

The Yeast Connection Handbook by William Crook, M.D.,
    Professional Books, 1996.
The Yeast Connection and the Woman by William Crook, M.D.,
    Professional Books, 1995.

enzymes ————————————

Digestive enzymes are proteins that help to break down food into small enough particles to absorb and use as fuel. High heat and other methods used during processing and cooking destroy enzymes. That's why it's better to eat most vegetables raw or lightly steamed. Plant enzymes are highly specialized.

- PROTEASE digests protein.
- AMILASE digests carbohydrates.
- LIPASE digests fat.
- CELLULASE digests fiber.

Eating a diet rich in raw foods keeps the body from having to work overtime compensating for the lack of enzymes. Since the body can't manufacture cellulase, plant foods are our only way to get it. Papaya[PP] (papain) and pineapple (bromelain) are excellent sources of enzymes. There are combination enzyme products on the market that are effective for a wide variety of foods. You may also want to have specific enzymes on hand for specific situations. A high-fat meal can be better handled with extra lipase. Avoid damaging your social graces after eating a meal of beans by making sure you supplement the meal with the enzyme that digests beans and legumes. And many people benefit from the enzymes that digest milk. Author and enzyme expert Terry Willard, Ph.D., estimates that seventy-five percent of his patients over age thirty are deficient in digestive enzymes.[5] Not only are you what you eat, you're what you can absorb from your food.

why fiber?

The importance of dietary fiber has been the subject of many recent studies. Some of the incredible feats of fiber are:[6]
- ◆ Lowers blood cholesterol.
- ◆ Stabilizes blood sugar.
- ◆ Prevents colon cancer.
- ◆ Aids in weight management.
- ◆ Removes certain toxic metals from the body.

Pretty impressive credentials. As a result of ingesting a high level of refined foods, Americans only get about twenty grams of fiber, just half of what we need. Whole grains, fresh raw vegetables, and most fresh fruit are good sources of fiber. Psyllium[PP] and slippery elm[PP] are good herbal sources.

types of fiber

When most people think of fiber, they think of *insoluble* fiber called roughage. This type of fiber provides bulk and promotes regularity since it doesn't break down during digestion. Insoluble fiber is found primarily in grains and beans as well as fruits and vegetables. Cellulose, hemi-cellulose, and lignin are insoluble fibers.

Soluble fiber is completely digested and absorbed in the small intestine. Pectin, mucilages, storage polysaccharides, and gums (like acacia or guar) are types of soluble fiber and tend to form gels that slow the absorption of nutrients (like sugar). Leveling out blood sugar is helpful for diabetics and those who have hypoglycemia.

parasites

> *"I strongly believe that every patient with disorders of immune function, including multiple allergies (especially food allergy), patients with unexplained fatigue, or with chronic bowel symptoms should be evaluated for the presence of intestinal parasites.)*
> Leo Galland, M.D., Townsend Letter for Doctors, 1988.

When we eat, our body sends signals to secrete the specific enzymes needed for that particular food. When we eat refined pseudofoods that are laden with chemical additives our body sends off signals to protect itself. Part of this protection is to secrete mucus into the intestinal lining so that the offenders are not absorbed as easily. Years of a diet loaded with pseudofoods causes a heavy mucus lining to build up. That mucus lining putrifies along with fecal matter that adheres to it to become an open invitation for parasites. We are continually exposed to parasites in our food and water. An unhealthy environment in the intestines allows the parasites to set up housekeeping.

No one wants to talk or think about intestinal parasites. But the problem is much more common than we realize and causes many health problems.

FURTHER READING

Guess What Came to Dinner, by Ann Louise Gittleman, Avery, 1993.

when trouble brews

When colon transit time, the balance of probiotics, enzymes, parasites, or a lack of fiber become a problem, trouble brews. The results are belching, gas, diarrhea, constipation, yeast infections, nausea, indigestion, heartburn, bad breath, diverticulitis, colitis, irritable bowel syndrome, and autointoxication—not a pleasant list of choices by anyone's standards. With eighty-five thousand cases diagnosed each year, colon cancer is one of the most common forms of cancer in the United States—and the numbers are growing.[7]

hot tips for good digestion

- ◆ Eat in a seated position in a quiet, pleasant environment without distractions.
- ◆ Eat your main meal at midday, when you have a sufficient amount of hydrochloric acid to digest your food and enough time for digestion before bedtime.
- ◆ Eat slowly so that your body produces enough digestive juice to handle your food without being overwhelmed.
- ◆ Avoid eating and drinking ice cold or very hot foods or beverages since they hamper the digestive process.
- ◆ Avoid beverages with meals to keep from diluting digestive juices.
- ◆ Eat a variety of foods for a variety of nutrients.
- ◆ Eat organic foods without chemical additives whenever possible.
- ◆ Chew food thoroughly (at least thirty times per average mouthful) to mix the food with enzymes in the saliva and to physically break down the food to the smallest particles for easier absorption. Savor the flavor.
- ◆ Increase the amount of raw vegetables, whole grains, and fruit in your diet for more fiber, enzymes, and other nutrients.
- ◆ Avoid antacids, which neutralize the hydrochloric acid needed for protein digestion.
- ◆ Only eat when you're hungry. More food stacked on top of undigested food compounds the digestive challenge.
- ◆ Combine food for the most efficient digestion.
- ◆ Eliminate when you have the urge. Don't procrastinate. And relax. Forcing the issue, so to speak, puts unnecessary stress on your body.
- ◆ Avoid coffee and non-herbal teas, even if they're decaf-

feinated. They contain acids, called tannins, that break down the natural sodium lining of the stomach. The result is that your natural stomach acids deteriorate the stomach lining as well as the food you eat.

♦ Exercising boosts metabolism and stimulates the muscular action in the intestines that causes a bowel movement.

♦ Drink eight glasses of water daily to provide the moisture needed for bowel movements.

♦ Limit dairy products which, in turn, will minimize mucus in the body. Whey, yogurt, and cottage cheese are the most easily digested dairy products.

♦ Limit refined foods such as white flour, white sugar, and white rice which will minimize mucus production and fermentation in the body.

♦ Substitute red pepper/cayenne/capsicum[PP] for black pepper (small amounts bring out the flavor of food without setting your mouth on fire. Black pepper is very hard to digest.)

♦ Eat the hardest-to-digest foods first, which allows your stomach's hydrochloric acid to work where it's the most needed. Remember, eat proteins first, salads last.

hot tips for cooking

♦ Avoid aluminum and non-stick cookware whenever possible (aluminum excesses have been linked to Alzheimer's and the chemical chips that constantly flake off of non-stick cookware don't count as fiber.)

♦ Eat forty to eighty percent of your diet raw so that you get enough enzymes and other nutrients.

♦ Lightly steam, broil, or bake your food to minimize nutrient loss.

♦ Avoid high-heated (especially fried) foods (oils cooked or processed at high temperatures, like hydrogenated oils, are chemically changed and hard for the body to digest).

♦ Because of margarine's hydrogenated oils and chemical

additives like artificial colors and flavors, butter is a better choice for cooking and eating. Cold pressed olive oil is an excellent choice for cooking and salads. Whenever possible, adding oils to your food after cooking keeps the oils from being heated at high temperatures.

◆ Cook all meat thoroughly, which minimizes your chance of swallowing a parasite or two.

waste management herbs ───────────

If you're like the vast majority of Americans, you're farther away from your goals for healthy eating, digestion, and elimination than you want to be. But don't give up. Until you can make progress in some dietary changes, there is herbal help. The herbs appearing in bold are most frequently used for the intestines, but the others can be very helpful, as well. Look for combination herbs that have those herbs appearing in bold lettering for your best bet for the intestines.

HERBS THAT ARE A GOOD SOURCE OF FIBER: **Psyllium**[PP], **slippery elm**[PP], chickweed, activated charcoal, and marshmallow.[PP]

HERBS THAT PROMOTE PERISTALTIC ACTION: **Cascara sagrada**[PP], **aloe**[PP], barberry, capsicum[PP], burdock, **senna**, and buckthorn.

HERBS USED FOR AN OVERGROWTH OF YEAST: **Garlic**[PP] and **pau d'arco.**[PP]

HERBS THAT HELP NORMALIZE PERISTALSIS (THROUGH STRESS REDUCTION): Lobelia[PP], valerian[PP], skullcap, chamomile[PP], and catnip.[PP]

HERBS USED TO CONTROL PARASITES: **Garlic**[PP], **artemisia**, black walnut, elecampane, cat's claw[PP], pumpkin seeds, **white oak**[PP], and **aloe vera.**[PP]

HERBS FOR INFECTION: Goldenseal[PP], **garlic**[PP], Oregon grape[PP], myrrh, and echinacea[PP].

final thoughts

A clean colon can mean the difference between good health and poor health; it will mean having boundless energy or barely enough energy to get through the day. We make the choice. Experiment with different foods for some pleasant surprises in taste. Whole foods are a pleasure to eat and very satisfying. When our bodies get the nutrition they need, they often lose the cravings for the things they don't need.

action plan

What are the steps you'd like to take in regard to improving your colon health?

_____

_____

_____

_____

_____

_____

_____

_____

_____

_____

_____

FURTHER READING

Prescription for Cooking and Dietary Wellness by Phyllis A. Balch, C.N.C. and James F. Balch, M.D., PAB Publishing, 1992.

Creating a Magic Kitchen by Dr. Bernard Jensen, Bernard Jensen Enterprises, 1981.

Food Enzymes:The Missing Link to Radiant Health by
Humbart Santillo, M.H., N.D., Hohm, 1993.

FOOTNOTES

1. Humbart Santillo, M.H., N.D., *Food Enzymes*, p. 42.
2. *Healthy!* (November 1996).
3. "Natural Digestive Enzymes," *Energy Times* (September 1996) p. 12.
4. John Robbins, *Diet for a New America*, p. 304.
5. Terry Willard, Ph. D., "Are you Still What You Eat?" *Healthy and Natural Journal,* 3, Issue 5, p. 42.
6. James F. Balch, M.D. and Phyllis A. Balch, C.N.C., *Prescription For Nutritional Healing,* p. 52.
7. Phyllis A. Balch, C.N.C. and James F. Balch, M.D., *Prescription for Cooking and Dietary Wellness,* p. 93.

the skin

t he largest organ of the body is the skin. It performs a variety of functions, such as protecting the body from physical damage, moisture loss and infection; insulating and regulating body temperature; housing sweat glands that eliminate acid wastes from the body; housing oil glands and nerve endings; and producing vitamin D from the sun's rays. Skin plays such an important role in eliminating waste from the body that it is often known as "the third kidney."

skin care

Taking care of your skin from the inside is even more important than taking care of it on the outside. Here are some ideas on keeping your skin healthy, inside and out.

- Drink lots of pure water to keep the skin hydrated and waste flushed out.
- Rest and avoid stress whenever possible.
- Exercise to sweat out waste and improve circulation to the skin. Interestingly, we sweat between two quarts and four gallons a day.
- Use natural, pH-balanced cleansers and moisturizers.

- ♦ Protect the skin from sun damage.
- ♦ Skin brushing sloughs off dead skin cells and steps up the circulation of blood and lymphatic fluid. Skin brushing is one of the most effective and least expensive ways to make a big difference in your health.
- ♦ Avoid antiperspirants which prevent the natural process of eliminating acid wastes through perspiration. Natural deodorants are fine. Some people find that with the use of chlorophyll, they no longer need deodorant.
- ♦ Wear natural fabrics like cotton, rayon, and linen that breathe and absorb moisture away from the skin.
- ♦ Avoid cigarette smoke which ages the skin.
- ♦ Avoid contact with harsh chemicals. There are many good organic cleansers on the market that will get rave reviews from your skin and the respiratory system.
- ♦ Improve circulation with aerobic exercise (like walking). Massage or herbs can also bring nutrients and health to the skin through the blood.

herbs for the skin

Does your skin look as young as you want it to look? Since your skin can be a reflection of your general health, any herb that strengthens the body will help the skin. But these herbs, in particular, nourish and care for the skin. The herbs appearing in bold are most frequently used for the skin, but the others can be very helpful, as well.

- ♦ ALOE VERA[PP] has been used for all types of burns, abrasions, hemorrhoids, inflammation, insect bites, rashes, and sores.
- ♦ EVENING PRIMROSE OIL is rich in essential fatty acids and has been used for all types of skin problems.
- ♦ **HORSETAIL**[PP] has been used externally for bleeding and skin rashes.
- ♦ IRISH MOSS is used for inflammation and dry skin.

- JOJOBA has been used by Native Americans to promote hair growth and has also been used for dry skin/scalp, dandruff, psoriasis, abrasions, acne, athlete's foot, eczema, seborrhea, and warts.
- **PAU D'ARCO**[PP] has been used for skin cancer, eczema, fistulas, fungal/bacterial infections, and psoriasis.
- SAGE has been used for sores (including mouth sores).
- **TEA TREE OIL**[PP] has been used topically for its antibacterial and antifungal capabilities for burns, candida, cold sores, infections (including staph and strep), and sores.
- YARROW[PP] is used to promote perspiration and for abrasions, burns, and cuts.

final thoughts

Taking care of your skin so that it stays youthful in appearance is important, but not nearly as important as keeping it healthy so that it functions well as the third kidney.

air supply:
the respiratory system

*"...disease is not the presence of something evil, but rather
the lack of the presence of something essential."*
Dr. Bernard Jensen

n one of us needs to be convinced of the importance of breathing. Being deprived of breath for just a few minutes can be fatal. Allergies, asthma, and other respiratory difficulties can make us miserable. The lungs, sinuses, pharynx, windpipe, diaphragm, and bronchial tubes are all part of the system that supplies oxygen to the tissues and removes poisonous carbon dioxide.

when good goes bad

Part of the body's natural process of survival is to keep the respiratory system clear so that we can breathe. When waste builds up as a result of assaults like air pollution, infection, cigarette smoke, and mucus-producing foods, our body is forced to produce large amounts of mucus to try to expel the blockages that prevent healthy breathing. The result? Coughs, sneezes, colds, flu, bronchitis, pneumonia, and more.

smoking

Over twenty-five percent of American adults are smokers.[1] With media coverage such as the recent television programs on class action lawsuits against tobacco companies, we're all painfully aware of the link between smoking and cancer. But lung cancer is only part of the damage done by smoking. Here are some examples:

- The healing of bones in smokers is considerably longer than in non-smokers.[2]
- The *Harvard Nurse's Study* found that women smokers are more likely to develop cataracts.[3]
- Children exposed to second-hand smoke run a greater risk of Sudden Infant Death Syndrome (SIDS), lung infections, and asthma according to the Centers for Disease Control and Prevention.[4]

Smoking kills more Americans each year than alcohol, cocaine, crack, heroin, car accidents, homicide, suicide, fire, and AIDS combined according to the American Cancer Society. Herbs that have been traditionally used to help smokers kick the habit are lobelia[PP], St. John's wort[PP], and hops.

air supply hot tips

The following tips are some ideas that have been used to help the respiratory system:

- Practice deep abdominal breathing techniques to increase the supply of healing oxygen to all parts of the body.
- Regular aerobic exercise can help breathing.
- During an asthma attack, a strong cup of caffeinated coffee* or cranberry juice has been used to open up the bronchial tubes until medical help can be reached.
- Avoid cigarette smoke.

* Caffeinated coffee can be very hard on the digestive, nervous, and circulatory systems but has been used in an emergency.

87

- ◆ Have lots of houseplants. Besides increasing your oxygen and decreasing your carbon dioxide, they're beautiful to have around.
- ◆ A daily walk in the fresh air and deep breathing exercises can do wonders for our oxygen levels, alertness, and our attitudes.
- ◆ Avoid drugs that suppress the typical coughs, congestion, and sneezing of a simple cold.
- ◆ Avoid indoor chemicals like cleaning supplies, perfume, and air fresheners. There are effective, natural alternatives.

air supply herbs

If you live in environmentally-challenged surroundings or need respiratory support for any reason, read on. The herbs appearing in bold are most frequently used for the respiratory system, but the others can be very helpful, as well. Look for combination herbs that have those herbs appearing in bold lettering for your best bet for the respiratory system.

- ◆ CRANBERRY[PP] has been used to open up the bronchial tubes in asthma or bronchitis.
- ◆ FENUGREEK[PP] has been used for respiratory congestion and infection.
- ◆ **LOBELIA**[PP] has been used for asthma, bronchitis, colds, congestion, coughs, croup, earache, ear infections, and lung problems (like infections).
- ◆ **MA HUANG (EPHEDRA)**[PP] is a Chinese herb used for centuries as a bronchial dilator and decongestant, and is used for asthma, bronchitis, and pneumonia.
- ◆ MARSHMALLOW[PP] is a soothing herb used for asthma, bronchitis, coughs, emphysema, lung congestion, sore throat, and sinus problems.
- ◆ MULLEIN[PP] has been used for asthma, lung bleeding, hoarseness, pleurisy, sinus congestion/infection, and tuberculosis.

◆ STINGING NETTLE is used for bronchitis and asthma.

◆ THYME has been used for a tonic and antiseptic for acute bronchitis, lung congestion, throat problems, and sinus infections.

◆ YARROW has been used for colds, flu and lung hemorrhage.

◆ **YERBA SANTA** has been used as a mild decongestant for asthma, bronchial congestion, colds, hay fever, coughs, flu, nasal congestion, and sore throat.

final thoughts

With increased air pollution and allergies, respiratory problems are on the rise. According to the American Lung Association, about ten percent of emergency room visits and hospital admissions in thirteen U.S. cities may be caused by smog. From 1972 to 1993, asthma deaths rose forty percent.[5] Natural health approaches like herbs that feed the respiratory system can help you breathe easier.

FOOTNOTES

1. Shankar Vendantam, "People's Lies May Explain Why Some Health Programs Fail," *Knight Ridder Newspapers, Daily News* (November 20, 1996) p. 5A.

2. "University Update," *Energy Times* (September 1996).

3. Michael Ryan, "Coming Soon-Better Health Care For Women," *Parade Magazine,* (November 9, 1997) p. 12.

4. "CDC: Smokers Often Light Up Around Kids," *Daily News Wire Service,* (November 7,1997) p. 2A.

5. Leslie Barker, *Dallas Morning News/Daily News* (October 14, 1996).

herbage
verbiage

the natural
first-aid kit

i f you've started a more natural approach to health, you may want to rethink what you keep on hand for life's unexpected urgencies. In this section you'll find ideas on some natural herbal remedies to have handy when pesky problems arise. Historical uses are listed for each remedy. These herbs are usually taken by mouth unless specified otherwise. The herbs are listed in order of their importance but you'll want to select the items for your kit based on the needs and the most common urgencies that come up in your household.

caution

Remember these ideas are presented as education only. They are not intended to replace the advice and care of a qualified health professional. Always seek the advice of a competent health care professional before treating any condition at home. Special caution should be exercised in the care of children, seniors, those in any weakened condition, and pregnant women. For more information, see the "Power Plants" chapter.

tea tree oil (leaf)

◆ Used topically for athlete's foot, bites and stings, burns, cold sores, cuts and scrapes, earaches, hives, rashes, sores, and toothache.

essential oil combination*

◆ Used topically for bites and stings, bruises, cold sores, cuts and scrapes, pain (especially muscle pain), respiratory congestion, and sores.
◆ Used as an inhalant for motion sickness and respiratory congestion.
◆ This combination can also be used in a vaporizer.

*Contains camphor oil, peppermint, and wintergreen.

homeopathic remedy for distress

◆ Even though this is not technically an herb, this remedy deserves an honorable mention on this first aid list. Homeopathic remedies use herbs in their preparation.
◆ Also used for the stress and anxiety caused by traumas such as fender benders and minor bicycle accidents.

aloe vera (leaf)

◆ Used topically for abrasions, bites and stings, burns (including chemical, radiation, and sunburns), earache, hemorrhoids, inflammation, and rashes.
◆ Used orally for constipation, heartburn, indigestion, and stomachache.
◆ Can also be used to clean wounds and sores.

papaya (leaf) ————————————

- ◆ Used internally for gas, indigestion, insect bites, and heartburn.
- ◆ Used externally for bites and stings.
- ◆ Contains papain, an enzyme that digests protein.
- ◆ Chewable tablets are used as breath/candy mints and even have a pleasant taste.

ginger (root) ————————————

- ◆ Used for childhood diseases, colds, colic, fevers, flu, gas, nausea, hives, indigestion, morning sickness, motion sickness, rashes, respiratory congestion, stomach upset, tonic, toothache, and vomiting.
- ◆ Also used in bath water for soothing hives and rashes.

cascara sagrada (bark) ————————————

- ◆ Used for constipation and coughs.
- ◆ Used to stimulate peristalsis in the intestines.

rose hips (fruit) ————————————

- ◆ Used for bites and stings, bruises, colds, earaches, fever, flu, heart, infection, respiratory congestion, and sore throats.
- ◆ Can also be used externally on bites, stings, and bruises.
- ◆ An excellent, non-acidic source of vitamin C.
- ◆ Vitamin C ascorbates or vitamin C with citrus bioflavonoids are also good forms of vitamin C.

peppermint oil (leaf) ————————————

- ◆ Used orally for heartburn, indigestion, gas, morning sickness, nausea, stomachache or cramps, stress, and vomiting.
- ◆ Also used as an inhalant for mental alertness, morning

sickness, nausea, and vomiting.
- ◆ Also used on the teeth as a breath freshener.
- ◆ Tastes great as a tea (a couple of drops in warm water).

activated charcoal

- ◆ Used orally for diarrhea, gas, overdoses of some drugs,* and as an antidote for some poisons.*
- ◆ Used as a paste to apply to bites and stings (including bee stings and brown recluse spider bites).

*Rely on activated charcoal in case of drug overdose or poisoning only on the advice of a qualified health professional.

capsicum (fruit)

- ◆ Used topically for bleeding, cold hands and feet, cuts and scrapes, infection, inflammation, muscle aches, and mouth sores.
- ◆ Used orally for indigestion, infection, muscle aches, and respiratory congestion.
- ◆ Used as a gargle for sore throats (will burn for a few seconds).

valerian (root)

- ◆ Used for headache, heart palpitations, hysteria, insomnia, pain (especially muscle pain), and stress.
- ◆ Can also be used topically for pain.
- ◆ Not chemically related to Valium.
- ◆ Not addictive.

lobelia (whole plant)

- ◆ Used topically on bites and stings, bruises, earaches, menstrual cramps, muscle pain/spasms, and stiffness.

♦ Used internally for earache, insomnia, menstrual cramps, muscle pain/spasms, stiffness, stress, and respiratory congestion.

white willow (bark)

♦ Used for eczema, fever, headache, inflammation, pain, rheumatism, stress, and ulceration.
♦ This is the herb from which the synthetic drug aspirin was derived and then synthesized.

garlic (bulb)

♦ Used internally for indigestion, infections, and sore throat.
♦ Can also be used as a gargle for sore throats and topically for infections.
♦ The oil is used for earaches and ear infections.

drawing black ointment

♦ This is a combination ointment that contains herbs like goldenseal[PP], chaparral, comfrey, and red clover[PP] in a base of olive oil and beeswax.
♦ Used topically for cysts, infections, splinters, and warts.

oregon grape (root)

♦ Used for poor appetite, eczema, indigestion, and infections.
♦ This is a gentler alternative to goldenseal[PP].

wild yam (root)

♦ Used for arthritis, colic, inflammation, menstrual cramps, and muscle spasms.
♦ Often used topically in a cream base.

conclusion

You'll be glad to have these remedies on hand when health emergencies appear. For more complete descriptions on how herbs can be used, see the next chapter on Power Plants.

RESOURCES AND FURTHER READING

Cynthia B. Olsen, *Australian Tea Tree Oil First Aid Handbook*, Kali Press, 1991.

Earl Mindell, *Earl Mindell's Herb Bible*, Simon and Schuster, 1992.

Steven Horne, *Natural Remedies for Common Health Conditions*, Tree Of Light Institute, 1995.

Steven Horne, *Sunshine Sharing*, Tree of Light Institute.

Louise Tenney, M.H., *Today's Herbal Health*, Woodland, 1992.

food for thought

Which of these herbs should my family keep on hand?

_____

_____

_____

_____

_____

_____

_____

_____

_____

_____

_____

_____

_____

power plants

there are thousands of herbs that have been used therapeutically for centuries across the globe. Some are used more frequently than others and are more readily available. This section briefly profiles single herbs that pack nutritional power. Included are some primary historical uses for them along with some information on research. These herbs are usually taken by mouth unless stated otherwise. Most herbs have quite a few uses, some of which are very different from each other in regard to the body system that is affected. For example, lobelia[PP] is very effective in building the respiratory, nervous, and structural (muscles) systems. Herbs are very different from drugs that target a very specific illness.

caution

These ideas are presented as education only. They are not intended to replace the advice and care of a qualified health professional. Always seek the advice of a competent health care professional before treating any condition at home. Suggested dosage amounts should be on each bottle of herbs along with other information, such as whether to take with or in between meals. Special caution should be exercised in the care of children, seniors, anyone who is seriously ill, and pregnant women.

a special note on pregnancy

Many references are made in this chapter to point out the need for caution during pregnancy. Throughout history, however, women have relied on herbs during pregnancy for nutrients that are critical for mother and baby. Many women have taken the herbs that have cautionary notes with positive effects during pregnancy, especially in herbal combinations in which only a small amount of the particular herb exists. Caution is always prudent during pregnancy, especially in a difficult pregnancy or in mothers with histories of difficult pregnancies.

FURTHER READING

Herbal Healing For Women by Rosemary Gladstar,
    Simon and Schuster, 1993.
Today's Herbal Health for Women by Louise Tenney, M.H. and
    Deborah Lee, Woodland, 1996.

how to use this chapter

Herbs in this chapter are in alphabetical order. If you are looking for herbs that have been used for a particular problem like bronchitis, or an area of the body like the prostate, check the index. Use the Systems Summary Appendix if you would like to review the herbs that feed a certain system of the body, like the circulatory system.

activated charcoal

- ◆ Used internally for cholesterol, overdoses of some drugs, intestinal gas, antidote for some poisons, and stomach cramps. (Rely on activated charcoal in case of poisoning or drug overdose only with the advice of a qualified professional.)

- Used as a paste for insect bites (including bee stings and brown recluse spider bites).
- A study published in the *American Journal of Gastroenterology* indicates that activated charcoal is effective for stomach cramps and gas.[1]

alfalfa (leaf & flower)

- Used for anemia, arthritis, blood purifier, breath freshener, diabetes, mental/physical fatigue, fluid retention, hemorrhages, kidney cleanser, nausea, pituitary problems, rheumatism, and stomach ulcers.
- Very rich in chlorophyll, enzymes, vitamins, and minerals.
- Alfalfa has demonstrated antitumor and antibacterial properties in clinical studies.[2]

algae (entire plant)

- Blue-green, chlorella, spirulina, and red marine are the most effective types of algae (see also "Kelp").
- Used for cancer, cholesterol, fatigue, indigestion, liver problems, and tumors.
- Provides more vitamins, minerals, and protein by weight than any other food.
- Rich source of iron that is sixty percent more absorbable than other iron supplements.[3]
- Spirulina is a rich source of easily digested protein (sixty-five to seventy-one percent) and has twenty-six times the amount of calcium as milk.[4]
- A group in India studied the effects of spirulina on pre-cancerous lesions and found that after a year, all lesions were eliminated in all forty-four subjects.[5]
- In a 1996 study, researchers stated that a water extract of spirulina called calcium-spirulan (Ca-SP) "is a potent

antiviral agent against both HIV-1 and HSV-1. Ca-SP can be a candidate agent for an anti-HIV therapeutic drug that might overcome the disadvantages in many sulfated poly-saccharides."[6]

◆ Yes, herbs can come from the sea.

aloe vera (leaf) ──────────────

◆ Used externally for abrasions, burns (including chemical, radiation, and sunburns), deodorant, hemorrhoids, inflammation, insect bites, rashes, scar tissue, and sores.

◆ Used internally for digestive inflammation and irritation, as a gentle laxative, and for tapeworms.

◆ Distilled or concentrated products should be avoided since some nutrients are lost or altered during processing. A high quality juice is yellow and sour/bitter.

◆ The gel has thickening agents to allow easy application.

◆ According to the *Journal of Dermatological Surgery and Oncology*, aloe vera has demonstrated a shortened healing time after facial dermabrasion (the removal of the top layers of skin to remove scars).[7]

◆ Avoid internal use for babies and during pregnancy.

bee pollen ──────────────

◆ Used for allergies (especially hay fever),* cancer, protection from common chemical pollutants and radiation therapy, cholesterol, fatigue, lack of concentration, longevity, stamina, and strength.

◆ A slow build-up on dosage minimizes the chance of allergic reactions.

◆ Rich in protein and considered "nature's most complete food."

◆ Bee pollen is rich in vitamin B12, which is unusual in plants. This makes bee pollen an excellent choice for vegetarians.

* Local bee pollen works best for allergies.

♦ Often used by athletes for energy, stamina, and strength.
♦ Bees are not harmed in the process of removing the flower pollen. They pass through screens that "dust off" and collect the pollen.
♦ Bee pollen significantly reduced the side effects of radiation therapy in patients at the University of Vienna.[8]
♦ In the *Journal of the National Cancer Institute*, bee pollen is reported to prevent the development of cancerous tumors in mice.[9]
♦ Another study from the University of Japan in Kyoto, Japan stated that "ten out of twelve cases [of BPH] showed improvement. Of the ten men who improved, three were in the first stage of hypertrophy, four were in the second stage, and three were in the third and most serious stage of the condition."[10]

bilberry (fruit) ─────────────

♦ Used for blood vessels, cold hands/feet, diarrhea, eyestrain, macular degeneration, night blindness, urinary tract infections, and varicose veins.
♦ In one study, eighty percent of the subjects taking bilberry had improved visual acuity and night vision.[11]
♦ In another study, subjects taking bilberry increased blood supply to the eye by seventy-five percent.[12]

black cohosh (root) ─────────────

♦ Used for arthritis, asthma, bronchitis, epilepsy, high blood pressure, hormone balance, lungs, symptoms of menopause, menstrual problems, rheumatism, St. Vitus dance, stress, and tuberculosis.
♦ Contains natural estrogen and is considered a safe sedative.
♦ Studies show that black cohosh is an anti-inflammatory[13] and effective in the treatment of high blood pressure.[14]
♦ Not used during pregnancy.

blessed thistle (whole plant) ───────

- ◆ Used for anorexia, as a blood purifier, for circulation, lack of concentration, digestion, headaches, heart, hormonal balance, lactation, liver problems, and memory loss.
- ◆ Research has shown that blessed thistle can strengthen the spleen and liver and reduce fevers (thought to be a result of inducing perspiration).[15]

butcher's broom (rhizomes) ───────

- ◆ Used for atherosclerosis, blood clots, cold hands and feet, hemorrhoids, inflammation, phlebitis, and varicose veins.
- ◆ Said to "sweep the veins and arteries clean."
- ◆ Research in Germany and France has indicated that butcher's broom reduces post-operative blood clots and provides measurable relief from hemorrhoids, varicose veins, and phlebitis.[16]

capsicum/cayenne (fruit) ───────

- ◆ Used internally for alcoholism, arthritis, bleeding, blood pressure balance, cancer, cholesterol, circulation, colds, diabetes, heart, indigestion, infection, inflammation, kidneys, muscle aches, respiratory congestion, rheumatism, strokes, tumors, and ulcers.
- ◆ Used externally for bleeding, cold hands and feet, cuts and scrapes, infections, inflammation, muscle aches, and pain.
- ◆ This is truly a shining star in the herb world. It is known as the purest and best stimulant. It also works as a catalyst to increase the power of other herbs and nutrients.
- ◆ Due to possible irritation, avoid using if hemorrhoids or kidney problems exist.
- ◆ Cayenne (red pepper) has been found to significantly decrease the pain of mouth sores at the Yale University Pain Management Center.[17]

◆ Studies at Yale University School of Medicine showed that capsaicin, a component of cayenne, prevented the growth of cancer cells in mice.[18]

◆ Cayenne fed to rats caused a significant reduction in triglycerides and cholesterol.[19]

◆ According to Charles Voight of the University of Illinois Department of Natural Resources and Environmental Sciences, "the painful heat sensation actually causes the body to produce endorphins, the body's natural pain killers."[20]

◆ The FDA has approved capsicum cream in the treatment of pain in post–shingles lesions.

cascara sagrada (bark)

◆ Used for cancer, constipation, coughs, gall bladder, indigestion, liver, and pancreas.

◆ Cascara sagrada means "sacred bark" in Spanish. Spanish settlers named the herb after being impressed with its effectiveness when used by the Native Americans.

◆ Clinical studies prove that cascara sagrada gently and effectively promotes peristalsis in the large intestine.[21]

◆ According to the *Journal of Clinical Medicine*, cascara sagrada contains a component that has strong antibacterial properties against harmful intestinal bacteria.[22]

◆ Use with caution during pregnancy.

catnip (whole plant)

◆ Used for colds, colic, convulsions, diarrhea, fevers, flu, gas, indigestion, and stress.

◆ A clinical study in Italy showed that catnip has antibiotic activity on stomach bacteria, which explains why it can provide gastrointestinal relief.[23]

cat's claw/uña de gato (inner bark) ———

- ◆ Used for cancer, candida, protection from the effects of radiation therapy and chemotherapy, chronic fatigue syndrome, intestinal problems (like Crohn's disease, diarrhea, diverticulitis, and irritable bowel syndrome), immune system, inflammation, joint problems, lupus, parasites, premenstrual syndrome (PMS), radiation, ulcers, and viruses.
- ◆ Clinical research shows that cat's claw reduces inflammation and acts as an antioxidant.[24]
- ◆ Not used for pregnant or nursing women.

chamomile (flower) ————

- ◆ Used internally for appetite stimulant, back pain, candida, diverticulitis, fevers, gas, hysteria, indigestion, insomnia, menstrual cramps, menstrual suppressant, sore throats (as a gargle), and stress.
- ◆ Used externally for abrasions, burns, cuts, and earaches.
- ◆ Often used for babies and children.
- ◆ Studies with mice indicate that chamomile relaxes nerves and eases gastrointestinal distress.[25]
- ◆ After dermabrasion, chamomile has demonstrated wound-healing capabilities in at least one study.[26]

chaste tree (fruit) ————

- ◆ Used for hormone balance, infertility, suppression of libido, symptoms of menopause (especially hot flashes), menstrual regulation, and PMS.
- ◆ Clinical trials indicate chaste tree decreases the symptoms of PMS.[27]
- ◆ Should not be used during pregnancy or in tandem with hormone therapy.

cranberry (fruit)

- Used for urinary tract infections and kidney problems.
- Studies show that cranberries make urine more acidic, reducing the likelihood of bacteria (*E. coli* is the most common) adhering to the urinary tract.[28]
- Almost all cranberry juice on the market contains refined sugar, which neutralizes most of the beneficial effects of the cranberry. Look for one hundred percent juice products, or use capsules, which have no sugar, or use fresh cranberries for eating or juicing.

damiana (leaf)

- Used for bronchitis, emphysema, fluid retention, hormone balance, impotence, hot flashes or other symptoms of menopause, Parkinson's disease, and sexual vitality.
- Research indicates that damiana increases sexual ability.[29]

dandelion (leaf and root)

- Used for anemia, arthritis, blisters, blood purifier, high blood pressure, blood sugar stabilization, cancer, cholesterol, eczema, gall bladder, kidneys, liver problems such as jaundice, and stamina.
- Helps to increase the flow of bile.
- The concentration of nutrients (even protein) makes this herb a good survival food.
- Current research indicates that dandelion is effective in the elimination of uric acid from the body and in the treatment of anemia.[30]

dong quai (root)

- Used for anemia, internal bleeding, blood purifier, brain nourishment, fatigue, female glands, fluid retention, hot

flashes and other symptoms of menopause, menstrual irregularity, and stress.
- Named the "queen of all female herbs" or "female ginseng."
- Dong quai has herbal precursors to estrogen according to clinical studies, which explains its use in normalizing female hormones.[31]
- Sometimes used during pregnancy.

echinacea (root)

- Used as a blood builder, for blood diseases, blood poisoning, blood purification, boils, cancer, immune system, bacterial and viral infections (especially colds and flu), lymph glands, prostate problems, respiratory problems, and vaginal yeast infections.
- Called the "king of blood purifiers."
- Studies have shown that an echinacea extract inhibits tumor growth (the *Journal of Medical Chemistry*) and a root extract destroys herpes and influenza viruses (*Planta Medica*).[32]
- A study in Germany at the University of Munich showed that echinacea increases the amount of T-cells (infection fighters) thirty percent more than immune-stimulating drugs.[33]
- In women with recurrent vaginal yeast infections, echinacea reduced the recurrence rate by forty-four percent.[34]
- Because of the potential to build up resistance to echinacea, some natural health professionals advise caution in regard to continuous use in large amounts.

elder (flower and berry)

- Used for allergies (especially hay fever), asthma, bronchitis, colds, mild diuretic (for fluid retention), fever, mild laxative, mucus, pneumonia, and sinus congestion.
- Often used with babies, children, and seniors.

◆ Clinical trials of elderberry in Israel during an outbreak of a flu virus showed a twenty percent improvement in symptoms in twenty-four hours, and ninety percent of the patients were cured within seventy-two hours (vs. no significant improvement until six days in the placebo group). The use of elderberry increased the number of antibodies, resulting in a higher level of immune response.[35]

eyebright (whole plant)

◆ Used as a blood purifier, for colds, eye problems (especially cataracts), inflammation, and liver stimulation.
◆ An infusion can be used as an eyewash.

fenugreek (seed)

◆ Used for bronchial and sinus congestion, cholesterol, lung (especially infections), mucus, and stomach irritations.
◆ Fenugreek has been shown to lower total cholesterol along with triglycerides LDL and VDL without affecting the "good" HDL.[36]

feverfew (leaf and flower)

◆ Used for arthritis, bursitis, colds, fever, migraine and sinus headaches, inflammation, and pain.
◆ A month of feverfew usage is generally required before improvement in migraine prevention and symptoms is realized.
◆ Avoid use in children under two or if pregnant or nursing.
◆ One study demonstrated a thirty-five percent decrease in migraines after taking feverfew for four months.[37]
◆ Thousands of arthritis patients were included in a study at the University Hospital in Nottingham, England, in which feverfew caused significant improvement in pain levels and range of motion.[38]

garlic (bulb) ─────────────

- ◆ Used for asthma, cancer immunity, cholesterol, ear infections, high blood pressure, indigestion, infectious diseases, lymphatic system, and intestinal worms.
- ◆ The oil is often used for earaches and ear infections.
- ◆ Unlike antibiotic drugs, garlic does not destroy the body's "beneficial bacteria."
- ◆ Also called "nature's antibiotic" and Russian penicillin.
- ◆ Avoid products that are odor–free or allicin–free since allicin is the component of garlic that kills bacteria and fungus. Concentrated products are available with a coating that dissolves in the small intestine (enteric coating), minimizing stomach upset and problems with your social life (as a result of the smell).
- ◆ Several studies indicate eating half a clove of garlic daily may decrease serum cholesterol by almost ten percent.[39]
- ◆ Researchers at Penn State University have found that twenty grams of garlic (about six medium size cloves) daily can reduce the incidence of breast cancer.[40]
- ◆ An Iowa study found that women who ate one or more servings of garlic per week had a thirty-five percent lower risk of colon cancer.[41]
- ◆ The National Cancer Institute published a study in 1989 reporting that those who ate the most garlic and onions were forty percent less likely to develop stomach cancer than those who ate the least.

ginger (root) ─────────────

- ◆ Used for childhood diseases, circulation, colds, colic, fevers, flu, gas pains, headache, indigestion, morning sickness, motion sickness, nausea, and toothache.
- ◆ Can also be used in the bath for hives and rashes.
- ◆ Combines well with other herbs and nutrients to enhance their effectiveness.

- One study here in the United States reported that ginger was more effective than over-the-counter medications for motion sickness and did not cause the drowsiness often associated with them.[42]
- A Danish study concludes that ginger can cause a significant decrease in the nausea and vomiting of morning sickness in pregnant women.[43]
- Should be avoided by anyone with bowel inflammations (like colitis, diverticulitis and irritable bowel syndrome).

ginkgo biloba (leaf)

- Used for alertness, allergies, Alzheimer's, asthma, attention deficit, blood clots, circulatory disorders (especially Raynaud's disease), dizziness, memory loss, stroke, and toxic shock syndrome.
- Recent studies in Europe have concluded that ginkgo helps prevent strokes through the prevention of blood clots.[44]
- In thirty-nine out of forty studies of ginkgo in Europe, a significant increase of blood flow to the brain was demonstrated, which improved problems with memory, absent-mindedness, and confusion.[45]
- Ginkgo has shown antiaging effects in geriatric rats.[46]
- Ginkgo has improved the memory and attention levels of Alzheimer's patients.[47]
- Another ginkgo study using an extract called *EGb 761* has demonstrated a reversal of symptoms in early Alzheimer's disease.[48]
- There are more than four hundred published studies and reports on *G. biloba* extract. It is the most prescribed herbal medicine in the world.[49]
- In a landmark decision, the American Medical Association endorsed *G. biloba* in October 1997 as a result of a study that demonstrated the delay of six to twelve months in the progression of dementia in one out of three Alzheimer's patients.[50]

ginseng (root)

- ◆ The three primary types of ginseng are Korean (or oriental), Siberian, and Wild American.
- ◆ Used for age spots, blood pressure, blood sugar balance, cold hands and feet, depression, endurance, hemorrhage, indigestion, longevity, vigor, sexual vitality, and stress.
- ◆ Called the "King of the Herbs" in the orient.
- ◆ Siberian ginseng is not technically a true ginseng but has some of the same properties.
- ◆ In a study of two hundred thirty-two chronic fatigue patients, all subjects experienced significant improvements after taking panax (oriental or Korean) ginseng.[51]
- ◆ It's best to avoid caffeine when taking ginseng.

goldenseal (rhizome and root)

- ◆ Used as an antiseptic, for appetite stimulation, internal bleeding, colon inflammation, convulsions, diabetes, flu, gastritis, infection (especially in the ears, teeth, gums and eye, or from giardia), liver problems, excessive menstruation, mouth sores, mucus, excessive perspiration, sore throat, and vaginitis.
- ◆ Not used during pregnancy or with high blood pressure.
- ◆ Not used if you have low blood sugar (myrrh can be substituted.)
- ◆ Known as one of the best therapeutic herbs in the plant kingdom.
- ◆ Berberine is a component of goldenseal that has shown antibacterial and antitumor capabilities by activating macrophages, therefore stimulating the immune system.[52,53]
- ◆ Less likely to cause stomach upset if taken in the middle of a meal.

gotu kola (whole plant)

- ◆ Used for alertness, boils, fatigue (mental and physical), high blood pressure, nervous breakdown, senility, stress, tonic, and vaginitis.

◆ Kola may sound like a soft drink, but there is no connection and no caffeine in gotu kola.

◆ Rats that were fed gotu kola for two weeks scored up to sixty times higher on tests of learning and memory than a control group.[54]

◆ Studies of mentally retarded children in India demonstrated an increase in IQ after taking gotu kola.[55]

grape (seed) ——————

◆ Used for strengthening capillaries, circulation, cholesterol, free radical scavenging (antioxidant), joint flexibility, phlebitis, and stress.

◆ High in proanthocyanidin (pycnogenol) concentration (more than ninety-five percent).

◆ Often combined with proanthocyanidins from the maritime pine tree (eighty-five percent concentration).

◆ In animal studies, proanthocyanidins have lowered blood cholesterol levels.[56]

◆ Proanthocyanidins are said to be the most powerful antioxidant: twenty times more powerful than vitamin C and fifty times more potent than vitamin E.

hawthorn (berry) ——————

◆ Used as an antiseptic, for hardening of the arteries, heart conditions (especially palpitations or an enlarged heart), blood pressure balance, hypoglycemia, insomnia, and stress.

◆ German researchers have conclusive evidence of the effectiveness of hawthorn in treating heart failure through lower pulse rates and more blood being pumped at a lower blood pressure.[57]

◆ Heart patients treated with hawthorn showed significant

improvements in heart rates and breathing compared to patients on a placebo drug.[58]

◆ Hawthorn can increase the effects of some prescriptions. Seek the advice of your health care professional to determine any potential interactions of hawthorn with drugs. As always, it's best to take drugs and herbs at least an hour apart.

horse chestnut (seed)

◆ Used for circulation, fever, and strengthening/toning veins (especially varicose veins).

◆ A study in Munich, Germany concluded that horse chestnut seed extract was as efficient in reducing leg swelling (due to lack of circulation) as was a diuretic combined with compression stockings (standard medical treatment).[59]

horsetail/shavegrass (whole plant)

◆ Used for internal bleeding, circulation problems, glandular disorders, brittle nails, nosebleeds, skeletal system (especially bone and cartilage repair), and urinary system (especially bladder problems, kidney stones, urinary ulcers, and suppressed urination).

◆ Research has shown that horsetail causes fractured bones to heal faster.[60]

◆ Should only be taken as recommended on the label due to the potential for excessive dosage to cause kidney impairment.

hydrangea (leaf and root)

◆ Used for arthritis, gallstones, gonorrhea, gout, inflammation, rheumatism, and urinary problems (especially infections, kidney stones and water retention).

◆ Hydrangea contains alkaloids which have cortisone-like action without the dangerous side effects.

juniper (berry)

- ◆ Used for bleeding, colds, infections, pancreas, uric acid build-up, and urinary problems (especially kidney infections and water retention).
- ◆ Juniper stimulates urine flow by increasing the rate of glomerulus filtration (which purifies the blood).[61]
- ◆ Not used during pregnancy.

kelp (whole plant)

- ◆ Used for adrenal glands, clearing arteries, colitis, complexion, eczema, fingernails, obesity, pituitary gland, and thyroid problems (especially goiter).
- ◆ Often used during pregnancy due to kelp's almost thirty different minerals (all the minerals considered essential to health).
- ◆ Sodium alginate, a derivative of kelp, can reduce heavy metal poisoning by as much as eighty-three percent.[62]
- ◆ Not recommended for those with high blood pressure due to the high sodium content of kelp.
- ◆ You're right. This is seaweed.

kudzu (fruit)

- ◆ Used for alcoholism and alcohol withdrawal. Researchers at Harvard Medical School found that kudzu reduced alcohol craving in animal studies.[63]

lobelia (whole plant)

- ◆ Used internally for alcohol withdrawal, arthritis, asthma, bronchitis, colds, congestion, convulsions, cough, cramps, croup, earache, ear infections, epilepsy, fevers, food poisoning, insomnia, lock jaw, lung problems, prevention of miscarriage, mucus, muscle pain, pneumonia, spasms, stress, tobacco withdrawal, whooping cough, and worms.

- Used topically for earache, menstrual cramps, muscle spasms, stiffness, and pain.
- Said to be the most powerful relaxant in the herb kingdom.
- Because of its strength and possible toxicity, lobelia is on the FDA's restricted list. Excessive amounts can cause nausea and vomiting. This herb, however, has been safely used for several hundred years even on newborn babies and seniors.
- Lobelia has been used as an expectorant based on its ability to stimulate the adrenal glands to release the corticosteroids that relax bronchial muscles.[64]
- This herb is usually taken at times of acute illness rather than on a daily basis.
- Used with caution during pregnancy.

ma huang/ephedra (whole plant)

- Used as a blood purification, bronchitis, bursitis, headaches, kidneys, venereal disease, and weight reduction.
- Avoid taking this herb in the late afternoon or evening. It can cause insomnia.
- Anyone who has high blood pressure, heart disease, diabetes, glaucoma, hyperthyroidism, or is pregnant or nursing should avoid this herb.
- Should not be combined with any form of caffeine.
- Ephedra has been used for thousands of years and is a safer alternative to ephedrine (a component of ephedra) or pseudoephedrine (another component of ephedra that is commonly used in over-the-counter sniffle medications).
- Several studies published in the *International Journal of Obesity* have proven that ephedrine makes it easier to burn fat through increased metabolism.[65]

marshmallow (root, leaf and flower) ───────────

- ◆ Used for asthma, boils, bronchial infections, coughs, emphysema, digestive irritation (especially diarrhea and irritable bowel syndrome) kidneys, lung congestion, sore throat, urinary bleeding, and infected wounds (internally and externally).
- ◆ In ancient times this plant was used to make marshmallows. The modern-day jet-puffed variety bears no resemblance nutritionally to the herb.
- ◆ Recent laboratory tests have shown that marshmallow has 286,000 units of vitamin A per pound, which explains how it can boost the immune system.[66]
- ◆ Marshmallow's ability to soothe respiratory irritations is well documented.[67]

milk thistle (seed) ───────────

- ◆ Used for alcohol withdrawal, boils, protection from the effects of radiation therapy and chemotherapy, gall stones, liver problems (especially cirrhosis), radiation sickness, and ulcers.
- ◆ Has been shown to lower cholesterol in the gall bladder (a precursor to gall stones).[68]
- ◆ Helps to prevent cirrhosis of the liver through the prevention of damage to red blood cells in the liver.[69]
- ◆ Helps to prevent ulcers (believed to be through antioxidant activity).[70]
- ◆ Clinical studies show that milk thistle has up to ten times more antioxidant activity than vitamin E.[71]

mullein (leaf) ───────────

- ◆ Used internally for respiratory problems (especially asthma, lung bleeding, bronchitis, coughs, croup, earaches, ear infections, hoarseness [as a gargle], pleurisy, sinus congestion/infection, and tuberculosis), bowel bleeding, diarrhea, insomnia, lymphatic system (especially tonsillitis), pain, and stress.

- Used externally for earaches and ear infections.
- Recent studies show that mullein contains saponins and mucilage which accounts for its ability to soothe and heal inflammation.[72]

oregon grape (rhizome and root)

- Used internally for poor appetite, blood conditions, indigestion, infection (especially staph), jaundice, liver and skin problems (especially acne, eczema, and psoriasis).
- Used externally for infections and skin problems.
- This is a more gentle alternative to goldenseal[PP].
- Studies have confirmed that Oregon grape is bacteriocidal due to high levels of berberine.[73]
- Not used during pregnancy.

papaya (fruit, juice and seed)

- Used for diarrhea, diptheria, gas, heartburn, indigestion, insect bites/stings, the intestinal tract, and stomach/duodenal ulcers.
- Contains papain, an enzyme from the green papaya that digests protein and is used as a meat tenderizer.
- Chewable tablets are used as a breath/candy mint and even have a pleasant taste.

parsley (leaf and seed)

- Used for bladder infections, breath freshener, blood builder and purifier, fluid retention, gallstones, jaundice, and kidney inflammation.
- Should not be used during pregnancy as it could bring on labor pains.
- Contains three times more vitamin C than citrus juices.[74]

◆ Often paired with garlic to make it more "socially acceptable."
◆ Used to dry up mother's milk after birth.
◆ Recent clinical trials show that parsley is antimicrobial (kills bacteria), lowers blood pressure, and tones uterine muscles.[75]

pau d'arco/taheebo (inner bark)

◆ Used internally for blood purification, cancer (especially leukemia), diabetes, bacterial and fungal infections (especially athlete's foot, candida, and herpes), and pain.
◆ Used externally for infections and pain.
◆ Lapachol, a component of pau d'arco, was found to have antitumor activity according to *Cancer Chemotherapy Reports*.[76]
◆ Dr. James Duke of the National Institutes of Health and Dr. Norman Farnsworth of the University of Illinois stated in the summary of their clinical trials that pau d'arco contains a substance effective against some cancers.
◆ Extracts of pau d'arco have reduced the growth of tumors in animals by forty-four percent in South American clinical trials.[77]

peppermint (leaf)

◆ Used internally for alertness, appetite normalization, colds, colic, fever, gas, heartburn, indigestion, irritable bowel syndrome, shock, sinus congestion, and stress.
◆ Used externally for alertness, fainting, fibromyositis, headaches, morning sickness, motion sickness, nausea, restlessness, rheumatism, stress, shock, and tendonitis.
◆ Tastes great and is soothing as a tea.
◆ The oil can be used on the teeth as a breath freshener, but beware: the oil is very concentrated.
◆ A study on the effect of enteric-coated peppermint oil on irritable bowel syndrome patients showed significant improvement in symptoms.[78]

red clover (flower) ——————

- ◆ Used for arthritis, blood purification, bronchitis, cancer, cysts, eczema, fluid retention, rickets, rheumatism, sores, sore throats (as a gargle), spasms, stress, and toxins.
- ◆ Often used for children and seniors.
- ◆ Research by the National Cancer Institute proves that four antitumor components exist in red clover.[79]

red raspberry (leaf) ——————

- ◆ Used for afterbirth pains, bowel problems, childbirth, diarrhea, female organs, fevers, flu, inflammation, to increase lactation, morning sickness, mouth sores, nausea, pregnancy, and vomiting.
- ◆ Often used for infants and children and during pregnancy.
- ◆ Research shows that using red raspberry "tones" uterine muscles (Relaxed muscles contract; in-tone muscles relax.).[80]

rose hips (fruit) ——————

- ◆ Used for bites and stings, blood purifier, bruising, cancer, capillary fragility, colds, earaches, fever, flu, heart, hemorrhoids, infections, sore throats, stress, and varicose veins.
- ◆ Contains sixty times as much vitamin C as oranges.

rosemary (leaf) ——————

- ◆ Used for a breath freshener, migraines, heart tonic, and stomach disorders.
- ◆ A study reviewed in *Cancer Research* showed that two constituents of rosemary—carnosol and ursolic acid—have inhibited skin tumors.[81]

rue (whole plant)

- ◆ Used internally for cramps, high blood pressure, hysteria, muscle cramps, strained muscles and tendons, neuralgia, sciatica, stress, and trauma.
- ◆ Used externally for strained muscles and tendons, muscle cramps, neuralgia, sciatica, and trauma.
- ◆ Studies performed on animals at the Chinese University of Hong Kong showed that rue lowers blood pressure.[82]
- ◆ Not used before meals since it may induce vomiting.
- ◆ Not used during pregnancy.

st. john's wort (whole plant)

- ◆ Used internally for after birth pains, AIDS, alcohol withdrawal, bronchitis, cancer, depression, skin problems, tobacco withdrawal, and viruses.
- ◆ Used externally for skin problems.
- ◆ Clinical trials show that St. John's wort is effective in treating mild-to-moderate depression without side effects.[83] A recent review of clinical studies in *The British Medical Journal* confirms these results.[84]
- ◆ Studies on mice indicate that St. John's wort is effective against viruses similar to HIV. On human HIV and AIDS patients, results have been inconclusive.[85]
- ◆ Yale-trained psychiatrist Harold Bloomfield is the author of *Hypericum and Depression*. He predicts that "hypericum [St. John's wort] is going to be the leading antidepressant" in this country. He believes we will follow Germany's lead, where it outsells all other antidepressant medications combined.[86]

saw palmetto (fruit)

- ◆ Used for digestion, glands (especially the prostate), reproductive organs, sexual vitality, and to increase weight.
- ◆ More than twenty double–blind placebo–controlled stud-

ies have shown that saw palmetto is very effective in relieving all major symptoms of benign prostatic hyperplasia (BPH) in men.[87]

- In many studies, ninety percent of the men studied experienced improvement in symptoms of BPH.[88]
- In one study of saw palmetto, nightly urinations were reduced by almost fifty percent and flow rates were increased by fifty percent.[89]
- Not used during pregnancy.

slippery elm (inner bark)

- Used internally for asthma, bronchitis, burns, colic, colitis, coughs, diaper rash, diarrhea (especially in babies), digestion, dysentery, lung problems, mucus, pneumonia, sore throats, tuberculosis, ulcers, urinary problems (especially kidney infections), and vaginal irritation.
- Used externally for burns, diaper rash, ulcers, and vaginal irritation.
- The FDA has approved slippery elm for sore throats and coughs.

suma (bark and root)

- Used as an antioxidant, for cancer, circulation problems, cholesterol, chronic diseases, fatigue, hormone imbalance, immune system, indigestion, stress, and viral infections.
- Sometimes called "Brazilian ginseng."
- Studies in Japan indicate that pfaffic acid, a component of suma, inhibits some types of cancers.[90]

tea tree oil (leaf)

- Used topically for boils, burns, candida, cold sores, infections (including staph and strep), joint pain, skin problems, and sores.

♦ Recent studies have shown tea tree oil to be effective against thrush, vaginal infections (*candida albicans*), staph, athlete's foot, and muscle/joint pain.[91]

thyme (whole plant)

♦ Used for alcoholism, asthma, athlete's foot, bronchitis, colic, fainting, fever, digestion, gas, infections, insomnia, parasites, throat problems, and warts.
♦ Not only does this herb bring compliments to the cook, it's a great therapeutic herb as well.

uva ursi/bearberry (leaf)

♦ Used for Bright's disease, diabetes, gonorrhea, menstrual problems, pancreas, prostate problems, spleen, urinary tract infections, and uterine ulceration.
♦ Large amounts should be avoided during pregnancy.
♦ Clinical trials have shown that an extract of uva ursi has some anticancer[92] and antibiotic capabilities.[93]

valerian (root)

♦ Used for heart palpitations, convulsions, high blood pressure, hypochondria, hysteria, insomnia, pain (used internally and externally), and stress.
♦ Currently the most widely used sedative in Europe.
♦ Valerian can act as a stimulant in hyperactive children.
♦ Valerian is not related to Valium.
♦ Not normally used during pregnancy.
♦ Not normally used for children (except in some cases of ADHD).
♦ Non-addictive, but not used for extended periods of time.
♦ Anyone currently taking sedatives or antidepressants should take valerian only under the supervision of a qualified health care professional.

- Unlike drugs used for anxiety, studies show that valerian does not impair the ability to drive or operate machinery.[94]
- Clinical studies have demonstrated valerian's ability to help patients get to sleep more quickly, have fewer night awakenings, and wake up without a "hung over" feeling and without the ability to concentrate (common side effects of sedative drugs).[95]

white oak (bark)

- Used for internal and external bleeding (especially in the urinary tract), menstrual problems, mouth sores, pinworms, skin irritations, teeth, sore throat (especially strep), and ulcers.

white willow (bark)

- Used internally for eczema, fever, headache, inflammation, suppression of libido, pain, rheumatism, and ulceration.
- Used externally for eczema, inflammation, pain, rheumatism, and ulceration.
- This is the herb from which aspirin was originally derived and synthesized.

wild yam (root)

- Used internally for arthritis, asthma, bowel spasms, breast problems (especially for fibrocystic tissue, tenderness, swelling, and to increase the size of small breasts), colic, gas, hot flashes and other symptoms of menopause, inflammation, liver problems, menstrual cramps, morning sickness, and PMS.
- Often used topically in a cream base for arthritis, breast problems, and menstrual cramps.
- Unlike synthetic progestins, the natural plant progesterones are safe.[96]

- One study done at Vanderbilt University on subjects with PMS had a ninety percent success rate using natural progesterone.[97]
- According to John R. Lee, M.D., his studies on the natural progesterone of the wild yam not only show improvement in symptoms of hormone imbalance (like PMS), but also "serial bone mineral density tests showed a significant rise without a hint of side effects."[98]

yarrow (flower)

- Used for blood purification, bowel bleeding, colds, fevers, flu, lung hemorrhage, measles, mucus, nosebleeds, and lack of perspiration.
- Often used for children, but should only be used by children over the age of two.
- Not used during pregnancy.

yucca (root)

- Used for arthritis, bursitis and rheumatism.
- Clinical research has shown that yucca lessens the pain, swelling and stiffness of arthritis[99] with the added benefits of decreases in high blood pressure, high cholesterol, and abnormal triglycerides.[100]

combinations vs. single herbs

Many combinations have been used over the years to build up certain systems of the body. There are combinations that have been used to strengthen the respiratory system, for example. Combinations are often the most effective choice for someone just beginning to use herbs for the following reasons:

◆ Because everyone's needs are different, a "shotgun" approach will probably be more effective and less expensive than trying individual herbs. The likelihood of getting the right herb for your needs is greater with combinations.

◆ The right combination of herbs, in the right proportions, work together "synergistically." The herbs work off of the nutrients in other herbs to make them more efficient all together than they would be individually. The total effect is greater than the sum of the parts.

final thoughts

The Chinese have used fifty-eight hundred plants with therapeutic properties over the centuries; twenty-five hundred have been used in India. We currently use less than one percent of all the edible plants on this earth. What a wealth of comfort and health exists for those who choose the natural approach!

REFERENCES AND FURTHER READING

Earl Mindell, *Earl Mindell's Herb Bible*,
    Simon and Schuster, 1992.
Louise Tenney M.H., *Today's Herbal Health*, Woodland, 1992.
Steven Horne, *Nature's Field*, Tree of Light Institute.
Kathi Keville, *Herbs: An Illustrated Encyclopedia*,
    Friedman, 1994.
Velma J. Keith and Monteen Gordon, *How To Herb Book*,
    Mayfield Publications, 1995.
Paul Barney, M.D., *Doctor's Guide to Natural Medicine*,
    Woodland, 1998.

food for thought ————

What areas of your health need some work (for example, the urinary system or stress)?

_____

_____

_____

_____

_____

_____

What herbs could address those needs?

_____

_____

_____

_____

_____

FOOTNOTES

1. "Activated Charcoal Provides Quick Relief," *Emerald Ladies' Journal,* May 1997.
2. E. Tyihak and B. Szende, "Basic Plant Proteins with Anti-tumor Activity," *Hungarian Patent 798,* 1970.
3. Steven Horne, "Super Algae," *Nature's Field.*
4. Steven Horne, "Spirulina, A High Protein Food," *Nature's Field.*
5. *Health* (March/April 1996).
6. Hayashi, J., et al. , "A Natural sulfated Polysaccharide, Calcium Spirulan, Isolated from Spirulina Platensis in vitro and ex vivo Evaluation of Anti-Herpes Simplex Virus and Anti-Human Immunodeficiency Virus Activities." *AIDS Res Hum Retroviruses,* 1996 Oct 10, (12):1463-1471.
7. Earl Mindell, R.Ph., Ph.D., *Earl Mindell's Herb Bible* (New York:Simon and Schuster/Fireside, 1992), p.38.
8. Steven Schechter, N.D., "Bee Pollen," *Co-Op Companion,* 3, No.3 (June 1994) pp.1-2.
9. Ibid.

10. Royden Brown. *Bee Hive Product Bible* (Garden City Park,New York: Avery Publishing Group, 1993), 52.

11. Steven Horne, "Bilberry Fruit Concentrate," *Nature's Field.*

12. Ibid.

13. P. S. Benoit, et al., "Biologic and Phytochemical Evaluation of Plants, XIV Anti-inflammatory Evaluation of 163 Species of Plants," *Lloydia,* 39 (2-3), 160-1, 1976.

14. A. R. Hutchens, *Indian Herbology of North America,* Norco, Ontario, Canada (1973).

15. Peter Holmes, *The Energetics of Western Herbs,* Artemis Press, Boulder, 1989, 278.

16. Steven Horne, "Butcher's Broom," *Nature's Field.*

17. *Prevention* (April 1996).

18. *Vitamin Retailer,* (February 1996).

19. Mindell, p.62.

20. Charles E. Voight, "Hot Pepper Foods," *Proceedings from the 3rd Annual Herb Winter Getaway Conference,* February 1998, p.189.

21. Michael Murray, N.D. and Joseph Pizzorno, N.D., *Encyclopedia of Natural Medicine.* Prima Publishing, Rocklin, California: 1991, 235.

22. M. Marchesi, et al "A Laxative Mixture in the Therapy of Constipation in Aged Patients." *Giornale De Clinica Medica.* Bologna, 63, 850-63, 1982.

23. L. D'Amico "Ricerche Sulla Presenza Di Sostanze ad Azione Anatibiotica Nelle Piante Superiori." *Fitoterapia.* 21(1) 77-79, 1950.

24. Louise Tenney, M.H., *Today's Herbal Health,* 4th ed., p.52.

25. *Townsend Letter for Doctors and Patients* (July 1996).

26. Brigitte Mars, "Calm Down With Chamomile," *Delicious!* (November 1995) p.52.

27. Propping, D. *Datzorke, Z. Allg* 1987; 63:932.

28. Tenney, p.66.

29. Alma R. Hutchens. *Indian Herbology of North America.* Merco, Ontario, Canada: 1969, 108.

30. N. R. Farnsworth and A. B. Seligman "Hypoglycemic Plants." *Tile and Till.* 57(3), 52-56, 1971.

31. *Murray and Pizzorno,* p. 462.

32. Mindell, p.84.

33. Steven Horne, "Echinacea Purpurea: Immune System Strengthener," *Nature's Field.*

34. Ibid.

35. Zakay-Rones, Z., et al, "Inhibition of Several Strains of Influenza Virus In Vitro and Reduction of Symptoms by an Elderberry Extract (Sambucus nigra L.)During an Outbreak of Influenza B Panama." *Journal of Alternative and Complementary Medicine* 1995; 1(4):361-369.

36. *HerbalGram* (Winter 1991).

37. Steven Horne, *Herbs Through the Seasons,* 1997.

38. "Feverfew: The Healthy Approach to Pain Relief," *The Healthy Cell News*, Fall/Winter 1993.

39. *Annals of Internal Medicine*, 119 (Oct.1, 1993), pp. 599-605.

40. *The Natural Way* (Aug/Sep 1995).

41. *Townsend Letter* (Feb/Mar 1996).

42. Jan Goodwin, "Healing Herbs," *New Woman* (May 1995) pp. 106-111.

43. *Townsend Letter* (April 1996).

44. Tenney, p.86.

45. *The Lancet*, 340 (Nov. 7, 1992): pp. 1136-1139.

46. *Townsend Letter* (Dec. 1994).

47. Steven Horne, "It's Not All In Your Head," *Sunshine Sharing 7*, No. 9.

48. *Townsend Letter*, Feb/Mar 1996.

49. *Natural Product Research Consultants*, "Ginkgo Biloba," ed. Donald Brown N.D.

50. Brigid Schulte, "Study: Chinese Herb Slows Onset of Alzheimer's Disease," *Daily News/Knight Ridder* (October 22, 1997) p. 6A.

51. *Townsend Letter*, July 1996.

52. Willard, T. *The Wild Rose Scientific Herbal*. Calgary, Canada, Wild Rose College of Natural Healing Ltd. 1991:253,299.

53. Tyler, V. *Herbs of Choice*. New York, NY: Pharmaceutical Products Press 1994: 162.

54. Steven Horne, "Improving Memory with Ginkgo and Gotu Kola," *Sunshine Sharing 7, No. 9*.

55. Ibid.

56. Michael T. Murray, N.D., "PCO Sources:Grapeseed vs. Pine Bark," *Health Counselor: Botanical Report*.

57. *HerbalGram* 34 (1994).

58. *Townsend Letter* (July 1995).

59. *The Lancet* 347: pp.292-294.

60. Tenney, p.96.

61. Daniel B. Mowrey, Ph.D. *The Scientific Validation of Herbal Medicine*, Keats Publishing, Connecticut, 1986, 83.

62. Steven Horne, "Kelp: Natural Mineral Source," *Nature's Field*.

63. *Proceedings of the National Academy of Sciences*, (November 1993).

64. Michael Murray, N.D., *The Healing Power of Herbs*, Prima Publishing, Rocklin, California, 1992, 241.

65. Shelley Beattie and John Romano, "The Ten Best Performance Supplements," *Muscular Development and Fitness*, July, 1995, 50, 192.

66. Jack Ritchason, *The Little Herb Enclycopedia*, 3rd Ed. Woodland Books, Pleasant Grove, Utah, 1994, 145.

67. R.W. Wren. *Potter's New Encyclopedia of Botanical Drugs Preparation*. 7th ed. Health

Science Press, Rustington, England: 1970.

68. *Hepatol* 91, 12:290-5.

69. *Life Sciences* 48 (1991): pp.1083-90.

70. *Journal of Pharmacy and Pharmacology* 44 (1992):pp.921-31.

71. Murray and Pizzorno, P.82.

72. "Mullein." *The Laurence Review of Natural Products: Facts and Comparisons, St.* Louis: September, 1989.

73. Mowrey, 57.

74. Ritchason, 163.

75. A. Y. Leung. *Encyclopedia of Common Natural Ingredients,* New York: 1980. 257-59.

76. "Early Clinical Studies with Lapachol," *Cancer Chemotherapy Reports,* Part 2, Volume 4, Number 4, December, 1974.

77. Rita Elkins, M. H. "Pau D'Arco" *Woodland Health Series,* Pleasant Grove, Utah, 1997, 17.

78. Michael T. Murray, N.D., "Clinical Uses of Peppermint," *Health Counselor.*

79. Steven Horne, "Red Clover:A Mild Blood Purifier for the Very Young and Elderly," *Nature's Field.*

80. Burns, J. H., et al, "A Principle in Raspberry Leaves which Relaxes Uterine Muscle" *Lancet* 2, 1941: 1-3: 6149.

81. Huang, M., et al, "Inhibition of Skin Tumorigenisis by Rosemary and its Constituents, Carnosol and Ursolic Acid," *Cancer Research* 1994: 54(2): 701-708.

82. Chiu, K.W. and Fung, A.Y., "The Cardiovascular Effects of Green Beans (Phaseolus aureus), common rue (Ruta graveolens), and kelp (Laminaria japonica) in rats," *Gen Pharmacol,* 1997 Nov, 29:5, 859-62

83. *Botanical Research Bulletin* 1 No. 3.

84. *British Medical Journal* (313:253-8) 1996.

85. Steven Horne, "St. John's Wort," *Nature's Field.*

86. Linda Sparrowe, "Nice 'N Spicy," *The Herb Quarterly Winter 1997,* P.3

87. Michael T. Murray, N.D., "Saw Palmetto:Nature's Answer to Enlarged Prostate.," *Health Counselor Magazine* 6 No.4 (1996).

88. Ibid.

89. Steven Horne, "Saw Palmetto:Relief from Symptoms Associated With Enlarged Prostate," *Nature's Field.*

90. Murray, Frank, "Suma Lauded," *Better Nutrition,* June 1987, p. 17.

91. James F. Balch, M.D. and Phyllis A. Balch, C.N.C., *Prescription for Nutritional Healing,* Garden City Park, New York; Avery Publishing Group Inc., 1990, 681,682.

92. J.L. Harwell, "Plant Remedies for Cancer," *Cancer Chemotherapy Reports,* July 19-24, 1960.

93. *Townsend Letter* (Dec. 1995).

94. R. Benigni "The Presence of Antibiotic Substance in the Higher Plants," *Fitoterapia*, 19 (3), 1-2, 1948.

95. Natural Product Research Consultants, *Valerian*, ed. Donald Brown N.D.

96. John R. Lee, M.D., *Natural Progesterone, the Remarkable Hormone*, revised (BLL Publishing, Sebastopol, California: 1993) p.16.

97. C.Norman Shealy, M.D., *DHEA: The Youth and Health Hormone*, Keats Publishing, New Canaan, Connecticut: 1986, 52.

98. Lee, 4.

99. Bingham,R.; Bellew, B.A.; Bellew, J.G. "Yucca Plant Saponin in the Management of Arthritis,"*J Appl Nutr* 1975;27(2-3):45-51.

100. Bingham, R. ,et al, "Yucca Plant Saponin in the Treatment of Hypertension and Hypercholesterolemia," *J Appl Nutr* 1978;30: 127-136.

other
natural health
approaches

introduction

"Yesterday is history. Tomorrow is a mystery. Today is a gift.
That's why we call it 'the present.'"
Anonymous

there are many different pathways to natural health. Herbs are one important option, but other options are gaining popularity as well. The alternative approaches described in this section of the book will allow you to know what choices exist so that you can make an informed decision in regard to your health and what's right for you. Additional options allow you also to form a partnership with traditional medical care for an integrated approach to health. Each approach has just a brief description, but with the further reading that is listed, you can pursue more detailed information on the methods that pique your interest.

"not invented here" syndrome

Americans are very proud of their heritage. Sometimes we take that pride to an extreme when it comes to health care. We sometimes feel that another country's approach to health care is not as advanced as our own. Such is the case with the acupuncture performed as part of Chinese medicine. In times past, acupuncture was considered to be at about the same level as voodoo. Now acupuncture is more accepted, especially in the area of pain management. So even if acupuncture was not invented here, it is slowly but surely being more accepted. We all need to learn the wisdom of the FIDO principle: Forget It and Drive On. Being open–minded can allow us to learn a great deal from other cultures, even if the other culture is here in the United States.

chronic diseases

In regard to emergency medicine and diagnostic technology, Americans have reason to be proud. But in the treatment of chronic diseases such as arthritis and diabetes, the present structure of standard medical care offers little relief. Research in the 1970s from the U.S. Department of Agriculture reports that forty-nine percent of our nation had one or more chronic conditions.[1] Despite progress in technology, cancer rates continue to grow annually. The incidence of cancer in the U.S. has grown from 635,000 cases in 1971 to 1,170,000 cases in 1993.[2]

what's in store

The other natural approaches in this section are:

- A "who's on first" list of types of practitioners that has information on credentials for different professionals in the natural health world.
- A brief description of a variety of natural health alternatives from Chinese medicine to juicing along with references to point you in the direction to learn more about each topic.

FOOTNOTES

1. C. Edith Weir, "Benefits From Human Nutrition Research", (Washington, D.C., USDA, 1971) p.60.
2. Charles B. Simone, M.D., *Cancer and Nutrition*, p. 3.

alternative health professionals

"Ask and it shall be given you; seek and ye shall find."
Matthew 7:7 KJV

With increasing numbers of people interested in the natural approach, new fields of alternative health care are cropping up. Some are old and familiar and making a comeback. Others are new. This section is devoted to making sense of all the options. Keep in mind that all numbers of practitioners are approximate.

acupuncturists and doctors of oriental medicine

WHAT THEY DO: Use fine, sterile, needles to rebalance energy centers throughout the body to restore health or prevent illness.

EDUCATION REQUIRED: Three years at an accredited college; two years science prerequisite

LICENSING: In thirty-one states (acupuncturists); two states (Chinese Medicine)

NUMBER OF PRACTITIONERS IN THE U.S.: 10,000

RESOURCE INFORMATION
American Association of Oriental Medicine
433 Front St.
Catasauqua, PA 18032
(610) 266-1433

ayurvedic doctors

WHAT THEY DO: Use body type and emotional make-up to design an individual program of diet and exercise.

EDUCATION REQUIRED: Five to six years of medical school in India (surgery allowed in India); no schools in the U.S.

LICENSING: None in the U.S.

NUMBER OF PRACTITIONERS IN THE U.S.: Possibly thousands practice, but just dozens are fully trained (B.A.M.S. degree)

RESOURCE INFORMATION
The Ayurvedic Institute
P.O. Box 23445
Albuquerque, NM 87192-1445
(505) 291-9698

chiropractors (D.C.)

WHAT THEY DO: Manipulate the alignment and balance of the skeletal system for proper nervous system function and the resulting health of organs.

EDUCATION REQUIRED: Two years of pre-professional college in biological science and four years residency at a chiropractic college.

LICENSING: All states and District of Columbia.

NUMBER OF PRACTITIONERS IN THE U.S.: 55,000

RESOURCE INFORMATION
Check your yellow page listings for chiropractors.
For more info on chiropractic:
American Chiropractic Association
1701 Clarendon Blvd.
Arlington, VA 22209
(703) 276-8800

herbalists

WHAT THEY DO: Provide information regarding herbs (prescribing is illegal).

EDUCATION REQUIRED: None (several alternative health colleges have herbalist programs).

LICENSING: None

NUMBER OF PRACTITIONERS IN THE U.S.: Unknown

RESOURCE INFORMATION
American Herbalist Guild
Box 1683
Soquel, CA 95073

homeopaths

WHAT THEY DO: Give minute amounts of herbal, mineral or animal substances to build the body's defense system.

EDUCATION REQUIRED: No formal guidelines or schools; usually 250-500 hours of education; naturopathic colleges allow a specialization in homeopathy.

LICENSING: Arizona, Connecticut, and Nevada

NUMBER OF PRACTITIONERS IN THE U.S.: About 3,000; 1,000 are M.D.s or D.O.s (Doctors of Osteopathy)

RESOURCE INFORMATION
National Center for Homeopathy
801 N Fairfax St. Suite 306
Alexandria, VA 22314
(703) 548-7790

naturopaths (N.D.)

WHAT THEY DO: Treat disease with a variety of techniques, such as herbs, homeopathics, raw glandulars, massage, and diet.

EDUCATION REQUIRED: Four years of naturopathic medical school.

LICENSING: In eleven states; efforts in progress in other states.

NUMBER OF PRACTITIONERS IN THE U.S.: 1,500 licensed or licensable; thousands more in states that require no licensing

RESOURCE INFORMATION
American Association of Naturopathic Physicians
2366 Eastlake Ave. East Suite 322
Seattle, WA 98102

osteopaths (D.O.)

WHAT THEY DO: Originally used joint manipulation to restore the structural balance of the muscles and skeleton. Osteopaths now are generally more aligned with traditional medical doctors.

EDUCATION REQUIRED: Standard medical training (four years of osteopathic medical school plus residency and internship).

LICENSING: All states and District of Columbia.

NUMBER OF PRACTITIONERS IN THE U.S.: 40,000

RESOURCE INFORMATION
American Academy of Osteopathy
3500 DePauw Blvd. Suite 1080
Indianapolis, IN 46268
(317) 879-1881

(w)holistic medicine doctors

WHAT THEY DO: In addition to prescribing natural and conventional medicine, work with the patient's emotional and spiritual states.

EDUCATION REQUIRED: Standard medical training (four years plus residency and internship).

LICENSING: All states and District of Columbia.

NUMBER OF PRACTITIONERS IN THE U.S.: 6,000 members of American Holistic Medical Association; perhaps 10,000 more M.D.s and D.O.s who practice some form of holistic medicine

RESOURCE INFORMATION
American Holistic Medical Association
4101 Lake Boone Trail Suite 201
Raleigh, NC 27607
(919) 787-5181

family doctors

When an alternative health care professional is not available or you're not quite ready for alternative care, don't forget the family doctor. A general practitioner is more likely to have a broader view of your overall health than a specialist. Like the famous psychologist Pavlov said, "If the only tool you have is a hammer, you're going to treat everything as if it were a nail." The more tools in the tool bag, the greater are our chances for success.

other natural health practitioners

Listed below are some other professional titles in the field of natural health that do not require licensing.

IRIDOLOGISTS analyze the iris of the eye to determine the body's strengths and weaknesses. Most iridologists are certified by natural health colleges across the country.

NATUROLOGISTS educate clients through lectures, testing, evaluation, and demonstrations to improve health. Naturology is a patented term that can only be used by the American Institute of Holistic Theology and its graduates.

NUTRIPATHS use nutrients to overcome disease. Nobel Prize winner Dr. Linus Pauling is an example of a nutripath who made tremendous breakthroughs with his work on vitamin C.

final thoughts

As you have seen, there are many choices when it comes to health care professionals and the partnership that you can establish when you want more than the average standard doctor's office visit of nine minutes. Some people believe that one avenue is the only answer. As is always the case, individuals must be assessed on their own merits and on compatibility regardless of the field they have chosen. Referrals from someone in the natural health world, like an herb shop or a health food store, may be your best option. Regardless of credentials, studies indicate that your success may vary to the degree to which you believe in your health care professional and that he/she believes in their own recommendations. We actually can mentally block an effective therapy and prevent it from working if we have no confidence in its effectiveness.

RESOURCES

Bill Thomson, "Looking For Dr. Right," *Natural Health* (Feb 1997).

Legal and Administrative Aspects of A Holistic Health Practice by
Chester P. Yozwick, N.D., P.M.D.,Ph.D.

Planning Your Career in Alternative Medicine by Dianne J. B. Lyons, Avery Publishing Group, 1997.

chinese medicine

"The greatest thing in this world is not so much where we are,
but in what direction we are moving."
D.W. Holmes

traditional Chinese medicine is staging a comeback both in China as well as in other parts of the world, including the United States. Acupuncture is probably the most easily recognized practice in Chinese medicine. But acupuncture is only a part of the system that views illness as a lack of harmony and balance in the body. Herbal remedies and a specialized massage called zone therapy are also important. In times past, Chinese doctors were only paid if their patients stayed healthy and were required to fly a banner of shame when a patient died. What an incentive system!

acupuncture

Acupuncture uses hair-thin needles inserted into strategic points on the body called meridians. These meridians correspond to the different organs or systems of the body and the flow of energy or ch'i. Chinese medicine says this process opens up these energy channels so that the proper life force can reach every part of the body. Western science claims that the process results in the release of endorphins that override pain information. According to *U.S. News and World Report*, twelve million people use acupuncture as a primary method of medical treatment.[1] Acupuncture is now licensed in thirty-one states and is sometimes covered by insurance.[2] According to the World Health Organization, stroke, infertility, bronchitis, flu, arthritis, dizziness, insomnia, and depression are included on the list of conditions responsive to acupuncture.[3] A National Institutes of Health panel concluded in 1997 that acupuncture is "clearly effective" for post-operative dental pain and nausea or vomiting from chemotherapy and anesthesia.[4]

FURTHER READING

The Complete Book of Acupuncture by Stephen D. Chang, Celestial Arts, 1995.

acupressure ────────────

This method uses the same theories and strategic points that acupuncture uses, but pressure is used instead of fine needles. The pressure of a finger is more palatable to most people, but finger pressure appears to take longer.

FURTHER READING

The Healing Benefits of Acupressure by F.C. Houston, D.C., D.D., Ph.D., Keats Publishing, 1991.

macrobiotics ────────────

The oriental approach to eating organically is called macrobiotics. This is not a strictly vegetarian diet. Some wild game and fish are included. The diet gained attention when Dr. Anthony Sattilaro, president of Methodist Hospital in Philadelphia, wrote Recalled by Life , the detailed story of his application of macrobiotics to help recover from what his doctors had called an "incurable cancer" that had metastasized to the brain, back and ribs. The diet Sattilaro used basically consists of:

- At least fifty percent whole grains
- About thirty percent raw and cooked vegetables
- Between ten to fifteen percent beans, sea vegetables and soups
- The balance in fruit and nuts (considered luxury foods)

FURTHER READING

Zen Macrobiotic Cooking by Michel Abehsera, Avon, 1976

final thoughts

Chinese medicine has withstood the test of time and is gaining new respect in the U.S.

FOOTNOTES

1. Karen Wolfe, "Pain," *Daily News* (March 13, 1997).
2. Bill Thomson, "Looking For Dr. Right," *Natural Health* (February 1997).
3. Carolyn Poirot, "Acupuncture Now Used to Treat Stroke, Asthma," *Daily News* (November 3, 1997).
4. Dick Thompson, "Acupuncture Works," *Time* (November 17, 1997) p. 84.

chiropractic

"The doctor of the future will give us no medicine but will interest his patients in the care of the human frame, in diet and in the cause and prevention of disease."
Thomas Edison

C hiropractic is a drugless, non-surgical relief from back and neck problems through spinal manipulation. Sound too good to be true? Over eight million American backs are suffering on an annual basis, and experts estimate that eight out of ten Americans will suffer severe, disabling lower back pain at least once during adulthood.

how does it work?

Through injuries like accidents, falls, and even the birth process that can be so traumatic to newborns, our spines can be out of alignment. When bones are twisted or misaligned in any way, nerves and blood circulation can be compromised. The nerves supply communication to and from the cells for information on how to function and heal themselves. It only makes sense that when these functions are impaired, problems can result. A chiropractic adjustment can manually realign the skeleton to restore the natural flow of the nervous system and circulation.

scientific studies ——————————

A three year study of seven hundred forty-one patients report-ed in the *British Medical Journal* in 1990 that chiropractic care was more effective for back pain and less costly that traditional medical care, short and long term.[1]

A 1993 study by the Ontario Ministry of Health concluded that common medical treatment has questionable value in the treat-ment of back pain and that chiropractic care is more effective.[2]

In 1979, a study commissioned by the government of New Zealand reported that chiropractic would have a positive influ-ence on the health of the nation and that chiropractic is remarkably safe.[3]

growing acceptance ——————————

An increasing number of American hospitals allow chiroprac-tors to treat patients in their wards and use hospital diagnostic equipment like X-ray machines.[4] The last ten years have been very different from times past when the American Medical Association ruled it unethical for its members to associate with chiropractors. Growing acceptance seems to be a result of law-suits, hospital economics, patient demands, and more accepting attitudes by a younger generation of doctors.[5]

federal guidelines ——————————

The U.S. Government recently issued federal guidelines for the treatment of acute low back pain. Key elements of the recom-mendation include activity modification, manipulation, and exercise.[6]

final thoughts ——————————

Many have found relief from serious muscle and skeleton problems with chiropractic care. As in all approaches to health, a partnership is critical. Exercises to strengthen the muscles so that the adjustment will "hold," good posture, and proper lifting techniques are practices that will help you hold up your end of the bargain.

FOOTNOTES

1. T.W.Meade, et al ,"Low Back Pain of Mechanical Origin: Randomized Comparison of Chiropractic and Hospital Outpatient Treatment," *British Medical Journal*, 300, 2 (June 1990) pp.1431-7.

2. Pran Manga, Ph.D., et al, *The Effectiveness and Cost-Effectiveness of Chiropractic Management of Low-Back Pain*, The Ontario Ministry of Health (August 1993) p. 104.

3. "Chiropractic in New Zealand," *Report of the Commission of Inquiry* (1979) p. 78.

4. *News Staff and Los Angeles Times,* "Chiropractors Finding An Adjustment of Attitude," *The Detroit News* (October 16, 1989).

5. Ibid.

6. *Rehabilitation of the Spine: A Practitioner's Manual,* ed. Craig Liebenson, D.C., p. 3.

colon cleansing

all those grandmothers were right: when you're sick, an enema can sometimes do wonders. As a preventive measure, cleaning the colon can rid the body of the tar-like buildup that lines the walls of the intestines. When we don't quickly eliminate the undigested food and metabolic waste that accumulates, fermentation results. We not only deprive our bodies of the nutrition we should have gotten from that food, we "autointoxicate" our bodies with the resulting poisons from fermenting foods. If you have any doubt about how harmful fermented food can be, check out that long-forgotten leftover in the back of the refrigerator and imagine how you'd feel after eating that! It has been said that death begins in the colon. Keeping it clean and functioning as efficiently as possible is crucial to overall health. Let's see what methods there are to cleanse this extremely important area of the body.

herbal cleansing

In general, plants help colon regularity and fruits are more cleansing than vegetables. Herbs like cascara sagrada[PP], capsicum[PP], and barberry are gentle cleansers. Senna and aloe[PP] are much stronger and are usually reserved for difficult cases.

colonics & enemas

Colon irrigation is done with water, but herbal extracts or juices can be added. A colonic is a more thorough enema that requires more user expertise, expert equipment, and more time (about an hour). Physiotherapists, chiropractors, or naturopathic doctors usually perform colonics. Get referrals or check the yellow pages of the phone book in most large areas under colon therapy.

final thoughts

Any cleansing can be taken to the extreme. Use good judgment and the advice of a professional before beginning a program. When we eat the right diet, we don't have the accumulation problems that necessitate a cleanse. But few of us eat the perfect diet and can often benefit from an occasional cleanse, which will result in renewed energy and a sense of well-being.

FURTHER READING

Tissue Cleansing Through Bowel Management by Bernard Jensen, D.C.,
    Ph.D., Nutritionist, Published by Bernard Jensen, 1981.
The Natural Way To Vibrant Health by Dr. N.W. Walker,
    Norwalk Press, 1972.
Become Younger by Dr. Norman Walker, D.Sc., Norwalk, 1978.

food combining

*"Unless you try to do something beyond what
you have already mastered, you will never grow."*
Ronald E. Osborn

the principles of food combining are based on the fact that your
body produces specific enzymes and levels of acidity to digest
specific types of food. For example, when you eat a baked potato, it triggers the production of an enzyme that specifically digests complex carbohydrates. When you eat a steak *with* the potato, the body
begins producing a different enzyme that targets the complex proteins
contained in steak. Suddenly, the conflicting environment in the stomach is worse than a bad soap opera and the digestion process slows considerably. When the food just sits there without being fully digested,
fermentation occurs (along with gas, bloating, and indigestion).

what combining works?

The rules of food combining can be very complex, but here are
some basic guidelines.

- THE MORE FOODS YOU EAT BY THEMSELVES, THE BETTER.
Variety is great, just eat one at a time when possible.

- WHEN EATING PROTEIN, EAT ONLY NON-STARCH VEGETA-
  BLES. There's a reason why you were up half the night after
  that steak and baked potato the other night. Most sand-
  wiches and the ever-popular hamburger on a bun are very
  difficult for the body to digest. Heaven only knows how
  long a hamburger with cheese and a bucket of fries fer-
  ments before escaping!

- EAT FRUIT BY ITSELF. It's best to not even mix different
  fruit together because of different acidity levels.

- ANY TYPE OF SUGAR MIXED WITH ANY OTHER FOOD CRE-
  ATES A SERIOUS FERMENTATION PROBLEM. Many people
  will have gas immediately after eating any sugar. Eating
  dessert with any meal can double or triple digestion time.

- FATS, COLD OR HOT FOODS AND DRINKS, AND LIQUIDS
  DURING MEALS SLOW DOWN THE DIGESTIVE PROCESS.
  More fermentation!

- INCREASE CONSUMPTION OF ENZYME-RICH LIVE FOODS.
  Forty to eighty percent of your food should be raw. Eat
  those veggies! Enzyme supplements also help, but food
  combining is the most effective approach.

digestion time table

Below is a list of foods and the time it takes to digest each one. Using this table lets you know whether you're combining or whether your food has already digested. *

FRUIT	1/2 HOUR
VEGETABLES AND HERBS	1 HOUR
WHOLE GRAINS, NUTS AND SEEDS	2 HOURS
FISH	2 HOURS
POULTRY	2-3 HOURS
BEEF	5 HOURS
PORK	7 HOURS

* Source: *Life Abundantly* by Ed Bashaw, p 47.

final thoughts

Even minor changes in the area of food combining can reap big rewards. Many people who "food combine" experience weight loss, are more alert, and are happy (along with their loved ones and co-workers) to no longer have a problem with gas.

further reading

Life Abundantly by Ed Bashaw, 1987.
Prescription for Cooking and Dietary Wellness by Phyllis A. Balch, C.N.C. and James F. Balch, M.D., PAB Publishing, 1992.

homeopathy

Samuel Hahnemann (1755-1843) was a highly respected German physician who was disgruntled with the ineffective medical practices of the time ("body friendly" practices like blood-letting, purging, and treatment with poisonous chemicals like mercury). He developed a system called homeopathy that worked with the body's own processes. Homeopathics often contain herbs in their preparation, but they are not related to herbs. Homeopathics, unlike herbal remedies, are regulated by the FDA and ninety-seven percent are available without a prescription. Homeopathics are very popular in Europe, where they have been trusted for over one hundred fifty years. The Queen of England retains a homeopathic physician for the royal family. One out of five U.S. doctors used homeopathy until the early part of this century when pressure from the American Medical Association and drug companies was the primary cause for the closing of most homeopathic colleges.[1]

how it works

Homeopathics work on the principle of "like cures like," similar to the principle used in vaccinations. A tiny amount of the offending substance rallies the immune system to fight the symptom(s). The word homeopathy comes from the Greek words *homoios* (similar) and *pathos* (suffering). Unlike drugs, which work against body processes to suppress symptoms, homeopathic remedies work with the body's immune system to attack the problem, all without side effects. Studies of the immune system are currently gaining momentum, partly due to the dramatic growth in auto-immune diseases such as AIDS and cancer.

safety

Homeopathics are so safe for children and adults that they have even been used every fifteen minutes for short periods of time until symptoms are improved or relieved. Since homeopathics are liquid, they're easier for children and pets to swallow than capsules. Homeopathics use alcohol in their preparation to prevent spoilage. If you want to avoid the alcohol, place the drops in a cup with three tablespoons of hot water. Let it stand for two minutes and slowly sip.

taking homeopathic remedies

Homeopathics can be a great complement to a drug prescription or herbs, but should be taken forty-five minutes before or after food (or anything with a strong aroma like coffee or peppermint oil). Follow instructions on the bottle carefully. If taking more than one homeopathic remedy, take them thirty to forty-five minutes apart for best results. Prescriptions are often very acidic and should be taken thirty minutes to an hour before or after any homeopathics or herbs to avoid diminishing the effects of the natural supplements. It's always best to consult your health care professional for advice in mixing anything (even food) with some prescriptions or over-the–counter medications.

final thoughts ———————

Homeopathic remedies are generally a safe, natural, inexpensive and effective option that works with your body's own processes. You can use them with confidence for symptoms as diverse as those involved with arthritis, stress, sinus problems, menopause, and premenstrual syndrome (PMS), just to mention a few. There are even homeopathics for appetite control and to help you quit smoking. A study of hay fever patients in Scotland showed that homeopathic remedies sharply reduced symptoms and the need for antihistamines.[2] Homeopathic remedies are experiencing a well-deserved resurgence, experiencing twenty-five percent growth annually.[3]

FURTHER READING

The Consumer's Guide To Homeopathy, by Dana Ullman, Putnam, 1995
Everybody's Guide To Homeopathic Medicines, by Stephen Cummings, M.D.
   and Dana Ullman, M.P.H., G.P. Putnam's Sons Publishing, 1991
A Beginner's Introduction to Homeopathy by Trevor M. Cook, Ph.D., Keats, 1990

FOOTNOTES

1. Andrew Weil, M.D., *Health and Healing,* p.23-4.
2. Jenny Gray, "Natural Remedies Battle Allergies," *Walton Sun* (October 4,1997) p. A25.
3. Phil Hall, "The State of Homeopathy in America," *Healthy and Natural Journal,* 3, Issue 3, p.114-5.

iridology

iridology is a science that may be completely foreign to many of us. It is used in many parts of the world as a very effective preventive health tool. Iridology is the study of the iris (yes, that blue, brown, green, or gray stuff in your eye) in regard to determining your body's particular strengths and weaknesses. A growing number of health food stores and herb shops are using iridology to develop individual nutritional/supplement profiles for their customers with a resulting increase in curiosity regarding the practice.

how does it work?

Even though iridology is a complex process, here is the "Cliff Notes" version of how it works. Every area of the body is reflected in nerve endings in the colored part, or iris, of your eye. When spots, discolorations, or other irregularities are identified in a particular part of the iris, it is correlated to a map-like grid

158

that indicates what areas of the body are strong and which ones are weak. (Iridology cannot, however, indicate a disease or illness exists.) For example, when the top outer portion of the iris is blurred or seems to fade into the white of the eye, circulation to the head area is not what it should be. If you can't remember where you put those keys or remember old what's-his-name's name more often than you'd care to admit, find a good magnifying mirror and check out your iris.

final thoughts

Many people are amazed with the accuracy of iridology and have enjoyed reading the many books available on the subject. It is fun to be an eye watcher. But the value in any analysis is what you do with the information. In the case of impaired circulation, many people will make a renewed commitment to exercise more or to work on their cholesterol levels. So as it turns out, the eyes are not only the window to the soul, they're also the window to good health.

FURTHER READING

Iridology Simplified by Bernard Jensen, D.C., Nutritionist, published by Bernard Jensen, 1980.

Visions of Health by Dr. Bernard Jensen, Avery Publishing, 1991.

juicing

"As we stand on the threshold of a new century, women are learning more than ever that they hold much of their health futures in their own hands."
Susan J. Blumenthal, M.D.,
Deputy Asst. Sec. for Women's Health,
Dept. of Health and Human Services

extracting juice from fruits and vegetables can be a great way to get concentrated nutrients to each cell of the body. The body quickly and easily uses the concentrated nutrients because it doesn't have to work hard to break down large particles to the size than can be easily absorbed. The body then has the energy needed to concentrate in other areas, like healing and "cleaning house" by getting rid of built-up waste. Juicing is often used for building immunity, increasing energy, and losing weight. When you feed the body the nutrients it needs, it doesn't crave more food, so it's a natural for controlling weight.

hot tips for juicing

- ◆ Vegetable juices tend to build the body; fruit juices cleanse. Going easy on the fruit can keep you from cleansing too quickly and overloading your elimination channels.

- Fruit juice usually contains a high level of sugar. Even though it is a natural sugar, be cautious not to overdo it.
- Carrots added to other vegetables in juicing helps to sweeten the taste.
- It's also helpful to follow the guidelines for food combining for the best results when juicing.
- Sip juice slowly and "swish" or chew the juice to stimulate the enzyme production that starts in the mouth.
- The juice is only as good as the produce from which it comes. So be sure to select fresh produce. Organically grown produce usually has a much higher level of nutrients than ordinary produce.
- An organic cleanser can be used on non-organic produce to remove some of the chemicals (like pesticides).
- Use a quality juicer that extracts a high percentage of the juice from the produce and uses filters for easier cleaning. Drink juice as soon as possible after preparation to avoid loss of nutrients.
- Carrot tops and rhubarb greens are toxic and should not be juiced.

Processed pasteurized juices have lost nutrients like vitamins, minerals, and enzymes. Natural unpasteurized fruit juices have made the news due to *E.coli* bacterial contamination from manure that was not washed from the apples. Juicing your own makes sense.

final thoughts

Juicing can be a great way to eat your veggies and get a power-packed dose of nutrients. Experiment with flavors and combinations for a real taste treat and a balanced variety of nutrients.

FURTHER READING

The Complete Raw Juice Therapy, Thorson's Editorial Board, HarperCollins Publishers, 1989.

Fresh Vegetable and Fruit Juices by N.W. Walker, D.Sc., Norwalk, 1978.

kinesiology

"Do not conform any longer to the pattern of this world, but be transformed by the renewing of your mind. Then you will be able to test and approve what God's will is – His good, pleasing, and perfect will."
Romans 12:2 NIV

One of the basic principles of natural health is the importance of listening to your body. One important way to listen to your body is to use applied kinesiology (a.k.a. biokinesiology, behavioral kinesiology, or muscle testing). You may have never heard of this science. If you haven't, here's a chance to learn about some incredible methods that are accepted in other parts of the world, and some parts of the U.S.

what is kinesiology?

Kinesiology is the science of anatomy, physiology, and mechanics of muscle movement. Applied kinesiology uses muscle strength and resistance as indicators of the food that it needs. The theory builds on the idea that your body is electromagnetic. Your electromagnetic field extends a few inches out from your body, as evidenced by the fact that when you approach a television screen, you often feel a static electricity charge from a few inches away. If you hold a substance within that electromagnetic field, it can make you a "stronger" or "weaker" circuit. Theoretically, if you're a stronger circuit, someone can test muscle resistance on any muscle and compare strength.

how does kinesiology work?

If you hold your arm out straight from your body and someone pushes your arm down, you can measure the amount of resistance either by the strength you feel, or by the use of a machine that precisely measures resistance. You then can compare the effects of holding different foods or supplements by holding them next to you. If a food makes you strong, your body is saying it needs that particular food. A weak response is your body's way of saying it does not need the substance.

who does kinesiology?

The procedure is not rocket science, but there are a few nuances. Experience and training are helpful if you want to get reliable results. Chiropractors and naturopathic doctors are often experienced in applied kinesiology as are an increasing number of herbalists. The procedure is also gaining popularity with doctors around the country. Many herb shops have employed kinesiologists and have been using the procedure with reliable results.

final thoughts

There are many vehicles on the road to good health. If we listen closely, they can tell us whether the engine is purring like a kitten or sputtering like a major tune-up is desperately needed.

FURTHER READING

Your Body Doesn't Lie by John Diamond, M.D., Warner, 1983.
The Ultimate Healing System by Donald Lepore, N.D.,
   Woodland, 1985.

skin brushing

"A wise man ought to realize that health is his most valuable possession and learn how to treat his illnesses by his own judgment."
Hippocrates

ooth brushing and hair brushing, yes—but skin brushing? If you haven't heard of skin brushing and don't indulge in it regularly, you don't know what you're missing. Brushing the skin with a dry, natural-bristle bath brush just before showering or after exercise can provide lots of benefits.

circulatory benefits

Increased circulation allows an increase of oxygen and nutrients to the cells, an increase in the elimination of normal cell waste, and increased cell production. Better circulation also helps you feel invigorated and alert.

lymphatic benefits

Lymph nodes are an important part of the immune system. Among other things, they act like little vacuum cleaners that rid the cells of waste and infection. Skin brushing helps to move lymphatic fluid so that the debris can be eliminated from the body through the circulatory system.

skin benefits

When the top layer of dead skin cells and residues from products like soap are removed, the skin can breathe better, feel softer and look better. When the pores are open, the normal daily process of eliminating two pounds of acidic waste from the skin is restored. Blemishes often disappear more quickly and skin color improves because acidic wastes like uric acid are no longer "trapped" under the skin.

how to skin brush

- ◆ Use a long-handled natural bristle bath brush. A pure vegetable bristle is best, but boar bristle is fine. A more gentle brush should be used on the face.
- ◆ Starting with the soles of the feet, brush the skin gently in circular motions up toward the heart until the lower body (except for the genitals) is completely brushed.
- ◆ Next, start at the fingertips and brush in circular motions toward the heart until the upper body is completely brushed.

final thoughts

The whole process is completed in less than five minutes and you'll feel like you've been pampered at an expensive spa. Your skin will tingle and feel soft and you'll feel more energetic, all without leaving the comfort of your home! It's a simple, very inexpensive way to make a difference in your health.

FURTHER READING

The Doctor-Patient Handbook by Bernard Jensen, D.C., Nutritionist, Bernard Jensen Enterprises, 1976.

miscellaneous methods

"Paralyze resistance with persistence."
Woody Hayes

aromatherapy

Science is now confirming what we've always known: scents can have a profound effect on our emotional and physical health. We all know the wonderful experience of smelling fresh-baked bread or a freshly cut evergreen. Essential oils have been used for centuries to treat disease, dress wounds, rejuvenate the weary, calm the frenzied, and prevent epidemics. These oils are generally used on the skin, or inhaled.

Aromatherapy is used today in Alzheimer's clinics, intensive care units, birthing rooms, dentists' offices, and during MRI scans. Lavender oil was used in the medical kit for soldiers in World War II for pain, convulsions, depression, inflammation, rheumatism, spasms, viruses, congestion, blood clots, fluid retention, and as a deodorant, antiseptic, and sedative—just to name a few. All that from a humble little blossom.

There are about forty oils being used today to treat everything from headaches and warts to depression and insomnia. Make sure the oil you purchase is natural, not synthetic. In 500 B.C. Hippocrates said that "The way to health is to have an aromatic bath and a scented massage every day."

ADDITIONAL RESOURCE

Gerrylyn Harvey, "Essential Oils Relax Mind, Rejuvenate Spirit," *Destin East!* (December 21, 1996).

FURTHER READING:

Magical Aromatherapy by Scott Cunningham, Llewellyn Publications, 1989.

ayurvedic medicine

This four thousand year old science of natural healing originated in ancient India. Its individualized approach to health is rapidly growing in the United States and in Europe. Ayurveda starts with determining your "dosha" or body/personality type to individualize treatment such as herbs and other foods. Exercise routines and relaxation techniques are also personalized to achieve physical, mental, spiritual, and emotional balance. Some Ayurvedic herbs are familiar like garlic[PP], ginger[PP], cloves, and nutmeg. Other herbs, like ashwaganda, are less well known. There are many Ayurvedic combinations that follow traditional formulas. Ancient Ayurvedic "pharmacists" studied the instincts of animals. During illness, they seek out certain plants that remedy their situation. Not only can we learn from other cultures, we can learn from the innate wisdom of the animal kingdom.

FURTHER READING

Perfect Health: The Complete Mind/Body Guide, by Deepak Chopra, M.D., Harmony, 1991.

A Beginner's Guide to Ayurvedic Medicine, by Vivek Shanbhag, M.D., N.D., Keats, 1994

fasting

Fasting has been used for centuries for religious as well as health reasons. There are many references in the bible to the benefits of fasting. Eating, digesting, absorbing and eliminating take up the vast majority of available body energy. When that energy can be diverted to healing and cleansing the body, your health can benefit either to maintain or improve health. One fasting technique allows only water. A more cautious approach is to take supplements and drink fresh vegetable and fruit juices during a fast. But fasting requires a great deal of caution. Pregnant or nursing mothers and children under eighteen should not fast. Someone with blood sugar problems, which are very common, generally does not do well during a fast. It's best to work with your doctor if you'd like to try fasting, especially if you have any serious health problems. Fasting is popular in Europe where there are hundreds of fasting clinics.

FURTHER READING

Juicing For Life, by Cherie Calbom and Maureen Keane. Avery, 1992.

Fasting Can Save your Life, by Herbert M. Shelton, American Natural Hygiene Society, 1993.

magnetic field therapy

Scientists have recently discovered what many ancient civilizations knew centuries ago: that external magnetic fields can effect the body's subtle internal magnetic fields. The use of magnets and controlled magnetic fields is growing. Magnetic resonance imagery (MRI) is replacing X-rays because of the increase in accuracy and safety.

External magnets are growing in popularity in treating imbalances in the body through the Hall Effect, which causes an increase in blood flow from an interaction of charged blood particles, resulting in a healing flow of oxygen and nutrients to a weakened or injured site.

According to William Philpott, M.D., an author and biomagnetic researcher, magnetic fields can stimulate metabolism and increase the oxygen available to cells without harmful side effects.[1] Robert Becker, M.D., an orthopedic surgeon and author, reports that weak electric currents promote the healing of bones.[2] Magnetic therapies show promise and seem to be used successfully in countries like Japan and Germany. One podiatric medicine college reported a fifty percent improvement in pain reduction and walking as a result of a study on heel pain and plantar fascitis using magnets.[3] It is estimated that ten million people in Japan sleep on magnetic pads for pain and insomnia.

The most common use of magnets is for pain management. The FDA has even approved an electromagnetic bandage that speeds the healing of broken bones.[4] Based on preliminary studies with a success rate of eighty percent, the Office of Alternative Medicine of the National Institutes of Health is sponsoring a study on the effect of magnets on pain. Additional studies on magnetic therapy are under way at Baylor College of Medicine, Tufts University, the University of Miami, Mount Sinai Medical Center, and the University of Kentucky.[5] Some concern exists regarding how each manufacturer produces the magnets in regard to the placement of magnetic poles and in regard to the direction in which they are placed on the body.

FURTHER READING

The Body Electric, by Robert O. Becker, M.D. and Gary Selden, William Morrow Publishing, 1985.

massage therapy ————

Massage therapy is not just for those who want to be pampered. In fact, it ranks third among the most frequently used alternative health approaches.[6] Services are often reimbursed by health insurance when prescribed by a physician. Massage can stimulate circulation and stimulate the flow of lymphatic fluid, which aids the immune response. Massaging the muscles not only helps them to relax and feel better, it also helps them to release the lactic acid build up that creates muscle aches. *USA Today* cited a study on the effect of massage on premature babies at the University of Miami School of Medicine. Massage resulted in forty-seven percent greater weight gain and six fewer days in the hospital.[7] Another study showed that massage can stimulate the body's natural painkillers.[8] Indulge. You'll be glad you did. Get referrals or check your yellow pages for "Massage Licensed Therapists."

meditation and prayer ———————————

Modern science is now validating what those who meditate and pray have known for centuries. Meditation and prayer is not only good for the soul, but also good for the body. Recent studies indicate that those who meditate can experience substantial decreases in blood pressure. Studies are so promising that the National Institutes of Health have allocated $3 million to further study the link.[9]

naturopathy ———————————

Naturopathic doctors (N.D.) are experts in holistic natural medicine. They use diet, herbs, other nutrients, mind/body techniques, homeopathy, and sometimes Ayurveda, but are restricted by law from prescribing. They often use hair analysis to determine body levels of minerals and poisons, and detailed blood analysis. Naturopathy has been around for centuries, but was introduced to the United States in 1902.

FURTHER READING

Encyclopedia of Natural Medicine, by Michael Murray, N.D. and Joseph Pizzorno, N.D., Prima, 1991.

reflexology

Reflexology is based on the Chinese zone therapy. It is the rubbing and pressure of zones on the hands and feet that correspond to other parts of the body. Pressure or rubbing breaks up the acid waste buildup that blocks the nerve flow or the flow of ch'i. Once the flow of ch'i is restored, circulation is restored, allowing healing through balance.

FURTHER READING

Stories the Feet Can Tell: Stories the Feet Have Told, by Eunice D. Ingham,
Ingham Publishing, 1984.

Hand and Foot Reflexology, by Kevin and Barbara Kunz, Prentice Hall, 1994.

therapeutic touch

The Journal of the American Medical Association states that the "importance of touch in medicine has been amply demonstrated...by nurse/healer Dolores Krieger".[10] As a professor of nursing at New York University, Dr. Krieger has started a tremendous resurgence in the ancient practice of healing touch. Her books and methods are used in nursing schools and hospitals across the country. Studies on the effect of her methods on objective measures (like electroencephalogram readings) are fascinating. Other similar methods are also gaining popularity, like "Touch for Health."

FURTHER READING

The Therapeutic Touch by Dolores Krieger, Ph.D.,R.N.,
Simon and Schuster, 1992.

Accepting Your Power to Heal by Dolores Krieger, Ph.D., R.N.,
Bear and Co., 1993.

Touch For Health by John Thie, D.C., T.H. Enterprises, 1987

vegetarianism

Our animals are fed increasing amounts of growth hormones and antibiotics in an effort to get them to the market faster. Many are very inhumanely treated and killed, which means the animals are in a state of dire stress with high adrenaline levels when they die. Ask a hunter how that impacts the meat when after being wounded, an animal will run in terror before dying. Hunters know that the adrenaline ruins the meat. At high levels, adrenaline is poison. Virtually all processed meat also has a high level of chemicals like preservatives. For these reasons and more, many Americans are minimizing or eliminating meat from their diets. Contrary to popular belief, you can get more than enough protein from vegetables and whole grains if you have the right information and plan carefully. Getting enough vitamin B12 for vegetarians can be accomplished with careful planning or natural supplements. There are several varieties of vegetarians:

VEGANS eat no animal food of any type.
OVO-VEGETARIANS eat eggs
LACTO-OVO-VEGETARIANS eat eggs and dairy products.

The New England Journal of Medicine reports that women who eat the most red meat are over twice as likely to develop colon cancer than those who eat the least red meat.[11] And the *Journal of The American Medical Association* reported in 1961 that a vegetarian diet can prevent ninety to ninety-seven percent of all heart disease.[12] A University of Iowa study showed that eating a lot of meat significantly increases a woman's risk of developing lymph node cancer. Women who ate more than 36 four to six ounce servings of red meat per month increased their chances of getting lymph node cancer by seventy percent over those who ate less than twenty-two servings per month.[13]

FURTHER READING

Diet for a Small Planet by Frances Moore Lappe, Ballantine, 1991.

Diet for a New America by John Robbins, Stillpoint, 1987.

final thoughts ──────────

Expand your horizons. Have fun exploring the possibilities. Maintain the right balance between open-mindedness and skepticism. You may find some pleasant surprises.

FOOTNOTES

1. *Alternative Therapies,* Ed. Larry Dossey, M.D. p. 334.

2. Ibid., p. 331.

3. Dr. Andrew Weil, *Self Healing* (November 1997) p.8.

4. American Broadcasting, *Good Morning America,* reporter Michael Guillen, Ph.D. (1995).

5. Karen Clark, "Chronic Pain: There Must be a Solution," *Healthy and Natural Journal* 44, Issue 6, p.100.

6. *New England Journal of Medicine* (January 28, 1993).

7. *A Guide To Massage Therapy in America,* The American Massage Therapy Association.

8. Karyn Feiden, "Medicine," *McCall's Health* (January 1997) p. 72.

9. *Energy Times* (April 1997).

10. Dolores Krieger, Ph.D., R.N., *Accepting Your Power to Heal.*

11. Phyllis A. Balch, C.N.C.and James F. Balch, M.D., *Prescription for Cooking and Dietary Wellness,* p. 145.

12. Ibid., p. 147.

13. "University Update," *Energy Times* (January 1996).

final thoughts

"Attend to your own inner health and well being. Happiness radiates like the fragrance from a flower and draws all good things toward you. Allow your love to nourish yourself as well as others. Do not strain after the needs of life – it is sufficient to be quietly alert and aware of them. In this way, life proceeds more naturally and effortlessly. Life is here to enjoy."
Deepak Chopra, M.D.

tragic and magic bullets

With the exception of serious accidents, deterioration of health is generally not caused by one "tragic bullet." A lifetime of exposure to polluted air and water, pseudofood, and stress accumulate and take their toll, a penny at a time, until we wake up one day with a serious health problem and don't know why. Just as there is rarely a tragic bullet, there is no "magic bullet" either. There is rarely a case where a lifetime of physical and emotional stresses on the body are wiped away. To ensure longer, happier lives, all of us need to plan ahead. You hopefully have a variety of ideas to implement at this point. Hopefully, you understand now that herbs can play an important part in achieving and maintaining optimal wellness.

change

Many individuals find that drastic change works for them. They are the ones who quit smoking or give up refined sugar cold turkey. Most of us, however, do better on a gradual plan to substitute and eventually eliminate. To eliminate soft drinks, for example, you may want to change to a natural soft drink, then later to juice, then later to juice diluted with water. Find what works for you. Be creative with your decisions every day to turn over a new leaf. Change can be a very pleasant journey.

are you alone?

Are you alone? Not by a long shot. Join the growing number of Americans who want the effective, natural approach to health. Maybe it's the mounting clinical evidence from all over the world. Whatever the reason, sixty million Americans spend $13.7 *billion* a year on alternative medicine.[1] The natural foods industry experienced a boost in sales of twenty-five percent in 1996 to $11.5 *billion*. And sales of vitamins and supplements increased 37.8 percent.[2] You're in good company.

choices

The body is a marvelous, complex organism that continually works to restore balance and heal itself. With knowledge, we have the power to make informed decisions that either support those processes or undermine them. We make choices every day, between developing new healthy habits and keeping old habits.

responsibility and reliability

Is there anyone who has as keen an interest in your health as you do? Certainly not any health professional, no matter how caring and competent they are. You are the one who takes responsibility and credit for making the decisions day in and day out that add up to health. But a wise person always seeks the counsel of experts. Take the opportunity to learn all that you can from a variety of reliable sources before you make decisions regarding your welfare. You'll be glad you did. We have more control over our health than the vast majority of us believe. There is a wealth of information available if we'll take the time to find it.

perseverance

Many individuals will try herbs or other natural health methods, see great improvements, then discontinue the program for one reason or another. Some quit soon after starting if they don't see immediate results. The "tyranny of the urgent" often steals from us the very things that are the most important to our health and well being. Prioritize your health needs. After all, think how much more you can be to yourself and to others when you have the physical, mental, and emotional energy that you need. And don't get discouraged by how far you have to go or slipping back into old habits. As long as you continue to improve your choices in life, a little at a time, don't beat yourself up over it. Set realistic goals and celebrate your improvement. You're worth the investment in time and effort. Turn your knowledge into action. Many people have taken before and after photos or have kept a journal to track their progress and determine what works and what doesn't work. Find what works best for you—but most importantly, keep at it.

seek out support groups

Finding others who are also learning to choose healthier paths can make the journey more fun. Check with herb shops and health food stores for activities. Many offer free classes on natural health topics and can be a wealth of information and support. Sometimes just one other person can provide a "buddy system" of support that can make a difference, like encouraging you to go for a walk when you were going to watch television instead. Stacks of books are available to you on natural health topics. Reviewing the choices outlined in this book can help you get started. And the section on alternative health professionals can give you some ideas for some support in that area. Health retreats are also growing in popularity and are a great source of information and support.

final, *final* thoughts

True health is learned and earned. It is not a gift, but a process of continuous improvement. Best wishes to you on your pathway to real health.

FOOTNOTES

1. "Small Bites:Alternative to What?," *Healthy and Natural Journal*, 4, Issue 6, p.59.
2. "News From the Field," *Healthy and Natural Journal*, 4, Issue 6, p.58.

getting there from here

My Personal Plan

What is my number one health challenge area?

_____

_____

_____

_____

_____

_____

_____

What herbs are the best choices for that challenge?

_____

_____

_____

_____

_____

_____

_____

What inherited weaknesses need strengthening?

_____

_____

_____

_____

_____

_____

What other health challenges are faced by my family (or loved ones)? What herbs are good choices for them?

_____

_____

_____

_____

_____

_____

_____

_____

What quick tips make the most sense for me to try to open up my:

Urinary System?

_____

Intestinal System?

_____

Respiratory System?

_____

Skin?

_____

What other natural health approaches would I like to pursue?

_____

_____

_____

_____

_____

_____

What books sound like interesting choices for me?

_____

_____

_____

_____

_____

_____

What are my goals (short and long range)? What are the target dates?

_____

_____

_____

My health professionals (Medical Doctor, Chiropractor,

Naturopath, etc.):

_____

_____

_____

_____

_____

_____

Signed

_____

Date

_____

systems summary

single herbs

CIRCULATORY

PURIFICATION: Alfalfa, Blessed Thistle, Butcher's Broom, Elderberry, Nopal, Oregon Grape, Red Clover, Yellow Dock

STRENGTHENING: Yerba Santa, Evening Primrose Oil, Flax Seed Oil, Garlic, Horsetail, Soy

CIRCULATION: Capsicum, Ginkgo, Gotu Kola, and Hawthorn Berries

DIGESTIVE

LIVER/GALL BLADDER SUPPORT: Barberry, Bayberry, Blessed Thistle, Burdock, Dandelion, and Milk Thistle

STOMACH/PANCREAS/SMALL INTESTINE SUPPORT: Capsicum, Fenugreek, Ginger, Oregon Grape, Milk Thistle, Papaya, Parsley, Peppermint, Rosemary, Safflowers, and Sage

GLANDULAR

HYPOTHALAMUS/PITUITARY/PINEAL SUPPORT: Bee Pollen

PANCREAS/ADRENALS SUPPORT: Korean Ginseng, Licorice, Nopal, Sarsaparilla, Siberian Ginseng, Wild American Ginseng, and Yohimbe

MALE REPRODUCTIVE FUNCTION SUPPORT: Chaste Tree, Damiana,

Saw Palmetto, and Yohimbe

FEMALE REPRODUCTIVE FUNCTION SUPPORT: Black Cohosh, Blessed Thistle, Chaste Tree, Damiana, Dong Quai, False Unicorn, Red Raspberry, Rue, Sage, Wild American Ginseng, and Wild Yam

THYROID SUPPORT: Black Walnut, Kelp, and Algae

IMMUNE

Black Currant Oil, Echinacea, Elderberry, Garlic, Goldenseal, Grape Seed, Morinda, Oregon Grape, Parthenium, Pau D'Arco, Rose Hips, Sage, Suma, Una de Gato (Cat's Claw), and White Oak Bark

INTESTINAL

CLEANSING: Black Walnut and Activated Charcoal

FLORA BALANCE: Artemisia, Garlic, Pau D'Arco, Pumpkin Seeds, Una de Gato (Cat's Claw), and White Oak

SOOTHING: Chickweed, Elecampane, Marshmallow, and Slippery Elm

TRANSIT: Aloe Vera, Barberry, Buckthorn, Burdock, Capsicum, Cascara Sagrada, Marshmallow, Psyllium, Senna, and Slippery Elm

NERVOUS

BRAIN FUNCTION SUPPORT: Blue Vervain and Sage

RELIEF/COMFORT: Capsicum, Feverfew, Grape Seed, Horse Chestnut, Rosemary, and White Willow Bark

CALMING: Catnip, Chamomile, Hops, Kava Kava, Kudzu, Lobelia, Passion Flower, Rue, St. John's Wort, Skullcap, Spirulina, and Valerian Root

VITALITY: Ginseng, Gotu Kola, and Ma Huang

RESPIRATORY

BREATHING: Yerba Santa

LOOSENING: Fenugreek, Stinging Nettle, and Thyme

SOOTHING: Fenugreek, Lobelia, Ma Huang, Marshmallow, Mullein, and Yarrow

SKIN AND HAIR
> GENERAL SUPPORT: Horsetail and Yarrow
> MAINTENANCE: Evening Primrose Oil, Irish Moss, Jojoba, Sage, Tea Tree Oil
> REPAIR: Aloe Vera and Pau D'Arco

STRUCTURAL
> BONE SUPPORT: Alfalfa, Flax Seed Oil, Horsetail, Red Raspberry, and White Oak
> CONNECTIVE TISSUE SUPPORT: Devil's Claw, Morinda and Yucca
> MUSCLE SUPPORT: Comfrey, Lobelia, and Rue

URINARY
> CLEANSING: Buchu, Cranberry, Licorice, Uva Ursi, and Yellow Dock
> ELECTROLYTE SUPPORT: Chickweed, Couch Grass, Dandelion, Juniper, and Siberian Ginseng
> ELIMINATION: Cornsilk, Dandelion, Hydrangea, Juniper, and Parsley
> SOOTHING: Bilberry, Horsetail, Marshmallow, Peach Bark, and Slippery Elm

VISION
> Bilberry and Eyebright

WEIGHT MANAGEMENT
> FAT METABOLISM: Chickweed
> THERMOGENESIS: Ma Huang

index